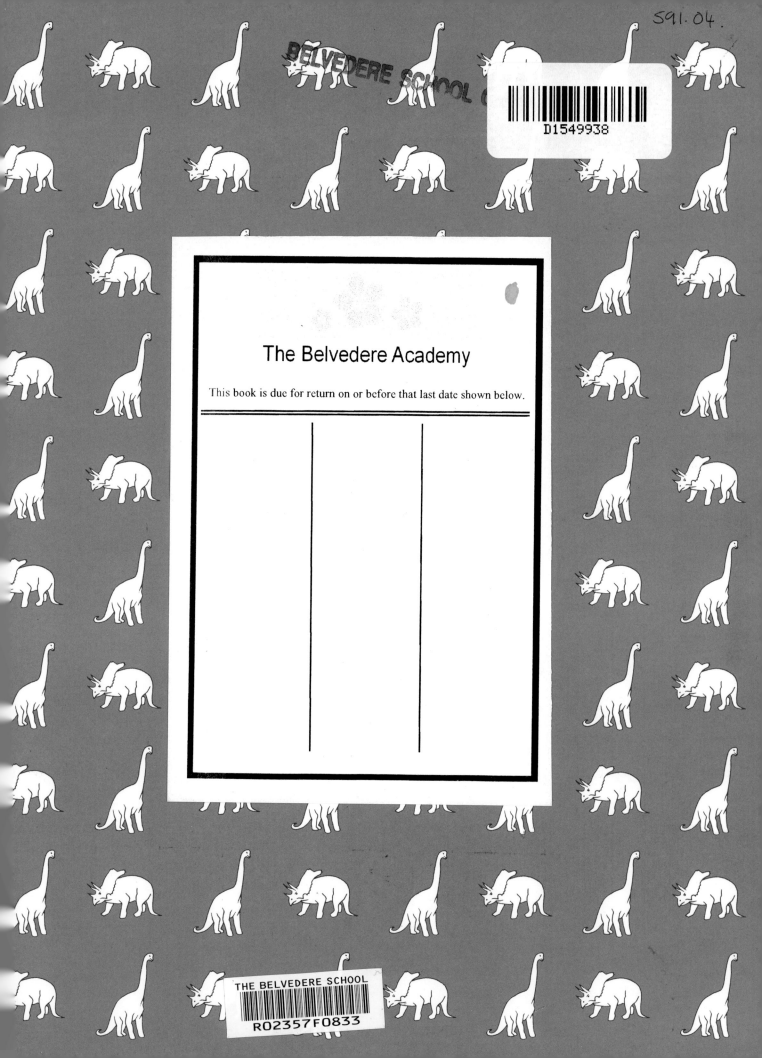

591.04.

D1549938

The Belvedere Academy

This book is due for return on or before that last date shown below.

DK EYEWITNESS GUIDES

DINOSAUR

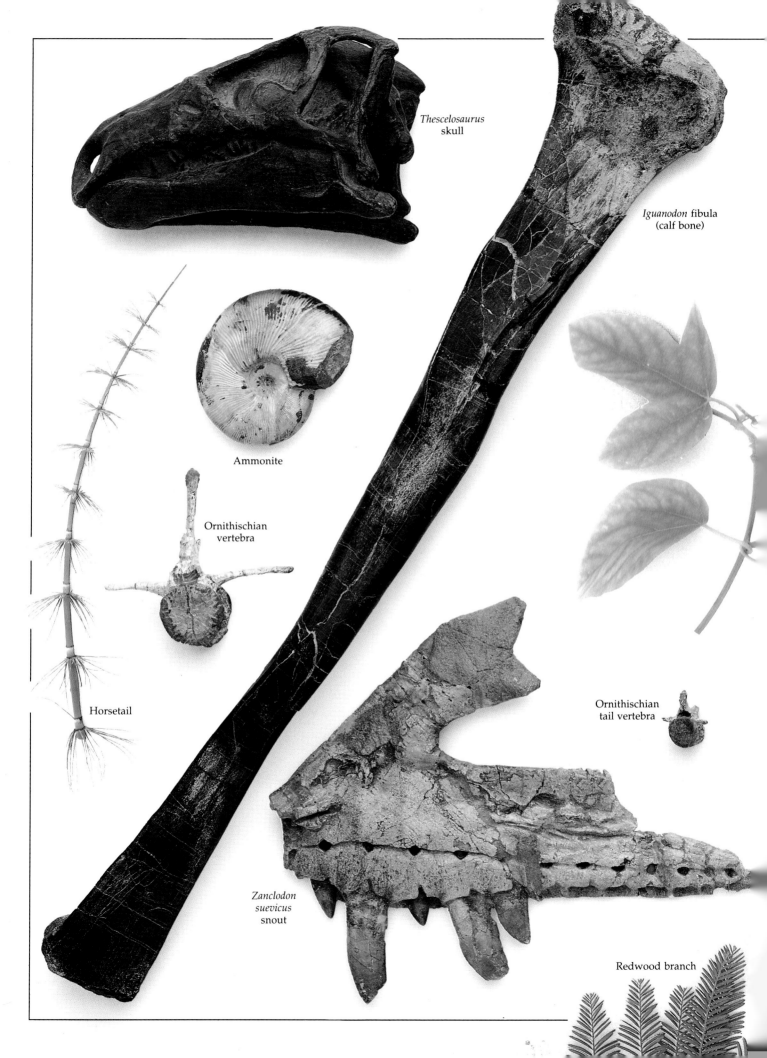

Thescelosaurus
skull

Iguanodon fibula
(calf bone)

Ammonite

Ornithischian
vertebra

Horsetail

Ornithischian
tail vertebra

*Zanclodon
suevicus*
snout

Redwood branch

Stegosaur tooth

Chirostenotes claw

Dogwood leaves

EYEWITNESS GUIDES

DINOSAUR

Written by
DR DAVID NORMAN
AND
DR ANGELA MILNER

Passionflower leaves

Gizzard stones

Cross-section of *Iguanodon* tail vertebra

Albertosaurus claw

Hadrosaur teeth

DORLING KINDERSLEY
London • New York • Sydney • Moscow
www.dk.com
in association with
THE NATURAL HISTORY MUSEUM • LONDON

Megalosaurus tooth

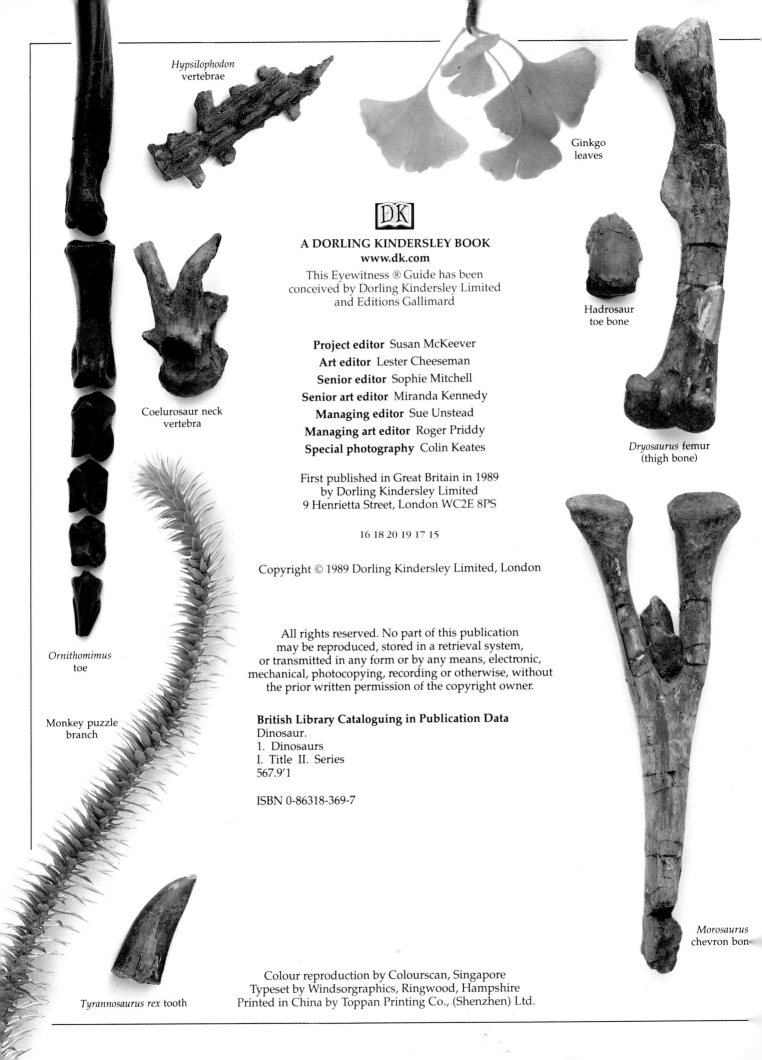

Hypsilophodon vertebrae

Ginkgo leaves

Coelurosaur neck vertebra

Hadrosaur toe bone

Dryosaurus femur (thigh bone)

A DORLING KINDERSLEY BOOK
www.dk.com
This Eyewitness ® Guide has been
conceived by Dorling Kindersley Limited
and Editions Gallimard

Project editor Susan McKeever
Art editor Lester Cheeseman
Senior editor Sophie Mitchell
Senior art editor Miranda Kennedy
Managing editor Sue Unstead
Managing art editor Roger Priddy
Special photography Colin Keates

First published in Great Britain in 1989
by Dorling Kindersley Limited
9 Henrietta Street, London WC2E 8PS

16 18 20 19 17 15

British Library Cataloguing in Publication Data
Dinosaur.
1. Dinosaurs
I. Title II. Series
567.9'1

ISBN 0-86318-369-7

Ornithomimus toe

Monkey puzzle branch

Tyrannosaurus rex tooth

Morosaurus chevron bone

Colour reproduction by Colourscan, Singapore
Typeset by Windsorgraphics, Ringwood, Hampshire
Printed in China by Toppan Printing Co., (Shenzhen) Ltd.

Contents

Heterodontosaurus skull

What were the dinosaurs?

BACK IN THE MISTS OF TIME, there lived an extraordinary group of animals. Called dinosaurs, they survived for nearly 150 million years, and then disappeared off the face of the Earth in the most mysterious extinction ever. Many of them were gigantic, but some were tiny, the size of a chicken. Some were peaceful and ate only plants; others were fierce sharp-toothed flesh eaters. Dinosaurs were reptiles, just like the living iguana lizard on this page. They had scaly skin and laid eggs. But unlike the lizard, which has short, sprawling legs, dinosaurs had long legs tucked under their bodies, which meant that they could move much more efficiently. Many other reptiles shared the dinosaur world, swimming in the sea and flying in the air, but dinosaurs lived only on land. We know about them today because their bones and teeth have been preserved in rock as fossils.

Tyrannosaurus rex
(lizard-hipped)

*Hip bones separate
(saurischian)*

Iguanodon
(bird-hipped)

*Hip bones next to
each other
(ornithischian)*

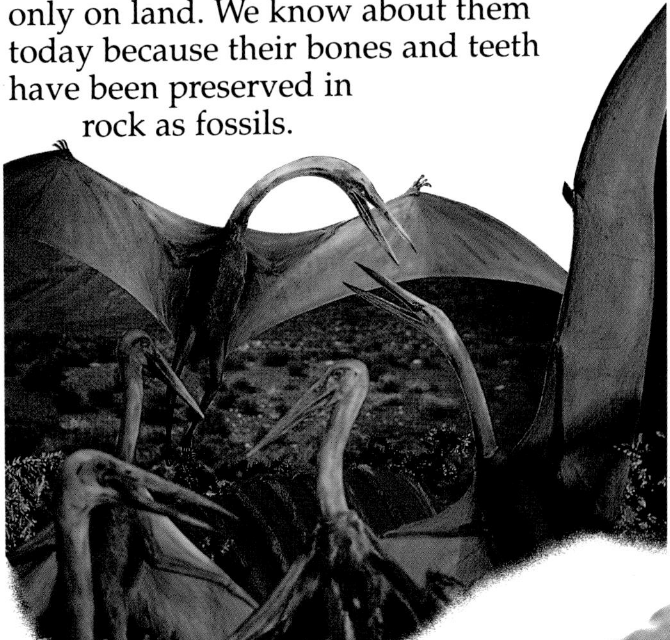

Iguana lizard

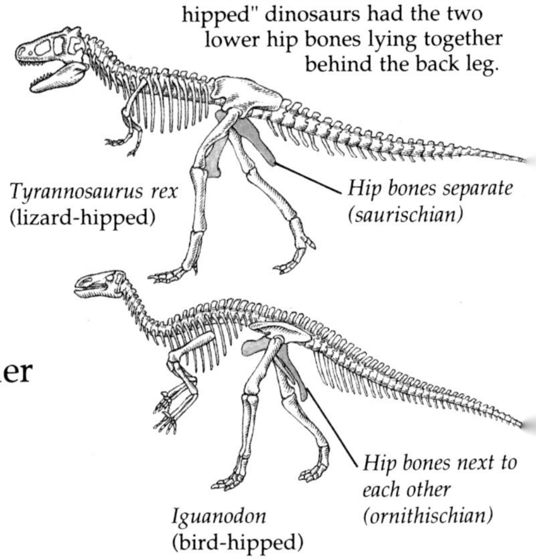

DINOSAURS COULDN'T FLY!
Flying reptiles, like the pterosaurs shown here feeding on a *Triceratops* carcass, shared the dinosaur world, but were not dinosaurs. No dinosaur could fly.

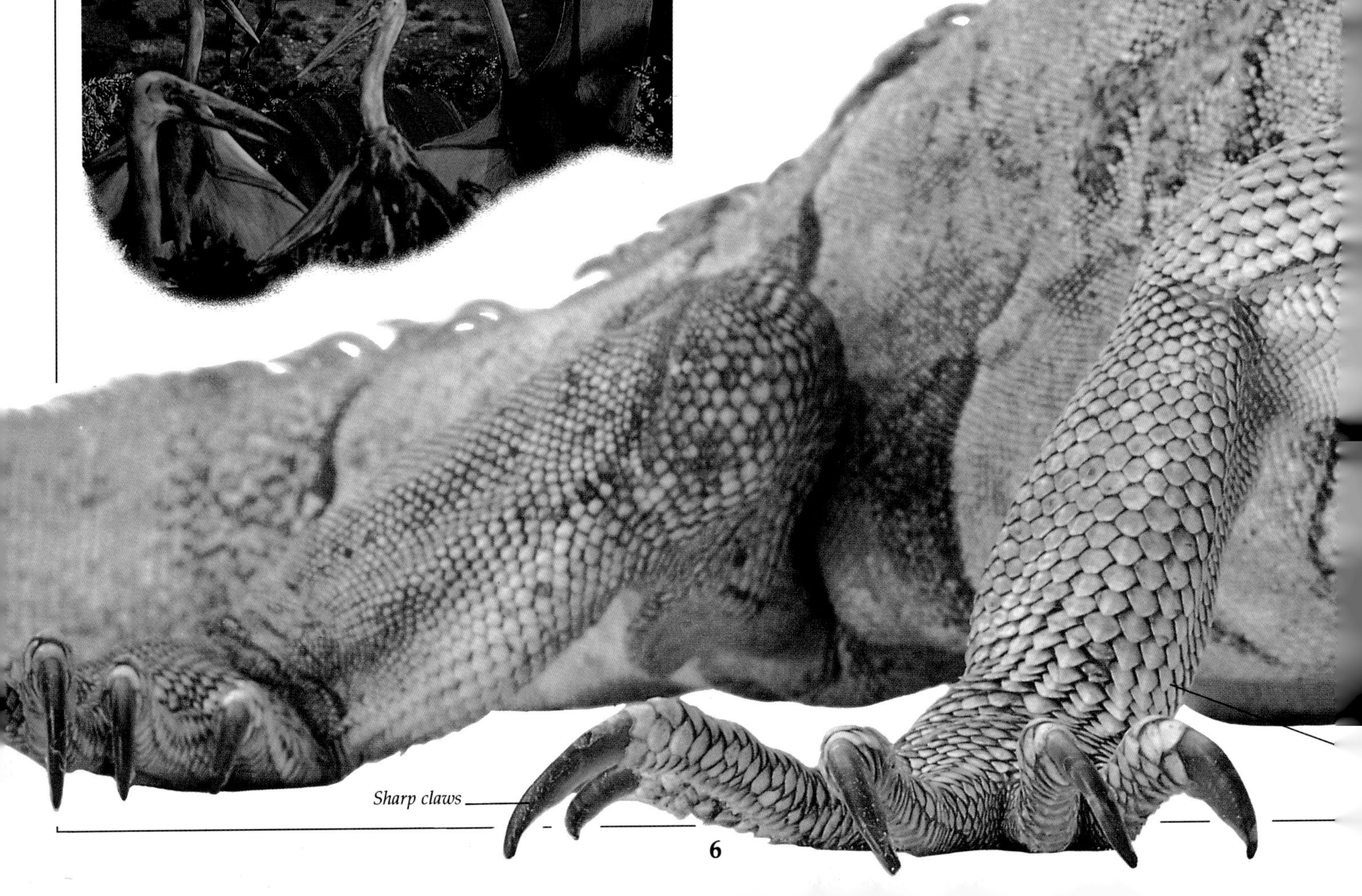

Sharp claws

6

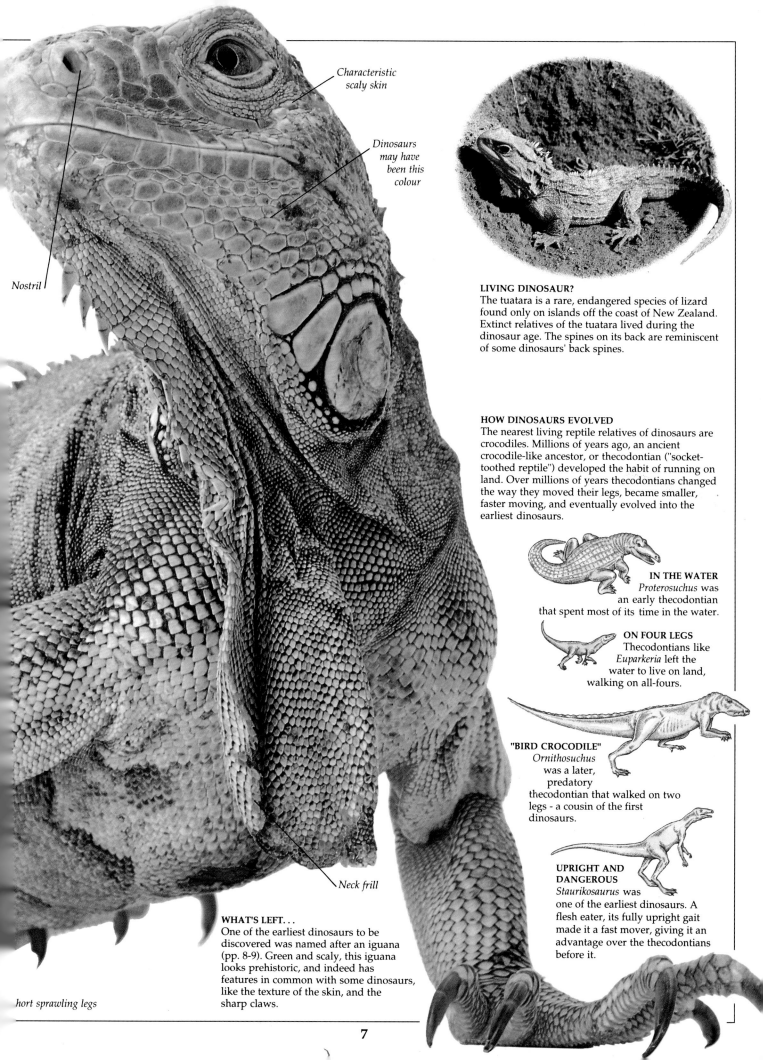

Characteristic scaly skin

Dinosaurs may have been this colour

Nostril

LIVING DINOSAUR?
The tuatara is a rare, endangered species of lizard found only on islands off the coast of New Zealand. Extinct relatives of the tuatara lived during the dinosaur age. The spines on its back are reminiscent of some dinosaurs' back spines.

HOW DINOSAURS EVOLVED
The nearest living reptile relatives of dinosaurs are crocodiles. Millions of years ago, an ancient crocodile-like ancestor, or thecodontian ("socket-toothed reptile") developed the habit of running on land. Over millions of years thecodontians changed the way they moved their legs, became smaller, faster moving, and eventually evolved into the earliest dinosaurs.

IN THE WATER
Proterosuchus was an early thecodontian that spent most of its time in the water.

ON FOUR LEGS
Thecodontians like *Euparkeria* left the water to live on land, walking on all-fours.

"BIRD CROCODILE"
Ornithosuchus was a later, predatory thecodontian that walked on two legs - a cousin of the first dinosaurs.

UPRIGHT AND DANGEROUS
Staurikosaurus was one of the earliest dinosaurs. A flesh eater, its fully upright gait made it a fast mover, giving it an advantage over the thecodontians before it.

Neck frill

WHAT'S LEFT. . .
One of the earliest dinosaurs to be discovered was named after an iguana (pp. 8-9). Green and scaly, this iguana looks prehistoric, and indeed has features in common with some dinosaurs, like the texture of the skin, and the sharp claws.

hort sprawling legs

Early discoveries

DINOSAUR MAN
This cartoon shows Sir Richard Owen, the man who invented the name Dinosaur. He is sitting astride a giant ground sloth (a fossil mammal that was found in South America).

Iguanodon tooth from lower jaw

Worn edge

Tooth from upper jaw

Aᴌᴛʜᴏᴜɢʜ ᴅɪɴᴏsᴀᴜʀ remains have been around for millions of years, people knew nothing about these extraordinary creatures until the last century. One of the first people to discover dinosaur bones was an English doctor called Gideon Mantell, who collected rocks and fossils as a hobby. In 1820 Dr Mantell, with his wife Mary Ann, found some large teeth embedded in stone. Mantell had never seen teeth quite like them before, and when he found some bones nearby, he began to do some serious research into the find. After a lot of work, Dr Mantell concluded that the teeth and bones had belonged to some kind of giant reptile, which he named *Iguanodon*, meaning "Iguana tooth"(pp. 6-7). Two other giant reptiles were discovered in Britain soon afterwards, named *Megalosaurus* and *Hylaeosaurus*. But it was not until 1841 that these creatures were given a group name. An eminent scientist of the time, Sir Richard Owen, declared that they should be called "Dinosaurs", meaning "terrible lizards". Thus began a time of great excitement in the scientific world. The great dinosaur hunt began all over the world.

THE FIRST TEETH
Still embedded in the gritty stone in which they were found by the Mantells, are the original *Iguanodon* teeth. The top edges of the dinosaur's teeth were worn down by chewing plants (pp. 26-27).

Horn on nose was actually a thumb spike

Long whiplash tail like an iguana lizard

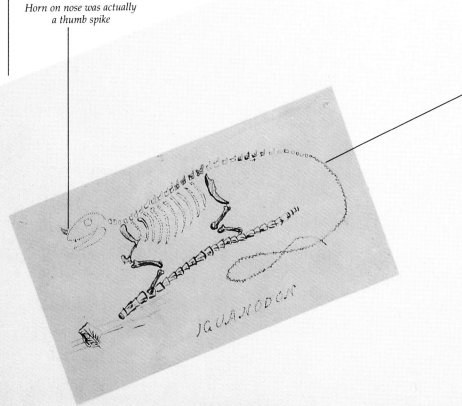

A ROUGH SKETCH
Dr Mantell had discovered a collection of bones and teeth. But what on earth had the owner of the bones looked like when it was alive? Mantell pictured it as a gigantic lizard, a bit like an iguana. He drew a picture of it perched on a branch, with its thumb spike (of which he had found only one) placed on its nose!

Gideon Mantell's original drawing of *Iguanodon*

Part of an
Iguanodon
backbone

Backbones fused
together

MYSTERY BONE
In 1809, long before the word
"dinosaur" had been heard
of, a man called William
Smith found some bones
in Sussex, England, in-
cluding this shin bone.
At the time, he did
not realize what they
were. Only later
were they ident-
ified as belonging
to *Iguanodon*.

THE DISCOVERER
Although he was a medical doctor by profession, Gideon
Mantell was an enthusiastic collector of rocks and fossils.
Soon his home looked like a museum as his collection grew.

DINNER IN A DINOSAUR
As the interest in dinosaurs grew, a great
display of giant models was mounted in the
gardens of London's Crystal Palace. Before the
Iguanodon model was finished, the sculptor
held a dinner party inside it for 20 people.

MORE BONES
More bones from *Iguanodon* found by Gideon
Mantell include this portion of the backbone
which fitted between the hips of the animal.

Iguanodon tibia
(shin bone)

MONSTERS IN THE PARK
These two concrete models of *Iguanodon* were made by the sculptor Benjamin
Waterhouse Hawkins in the last century. Although inaccurate - *Iguanodon* looked nothing
like this (p. 39) - they can be seen to this day in the park at Crystal Palace, London.

Dinosaur landscape

Monkey puzzle:
Araucaria araucana

DINOSAURS LIVED on the Earth for nearly 150 million years, and it is not surprising that their world changed substantially during this time. Continents, at first just one great landmass, gradually drifted apart until they resembled the modern arrangement that we are familiar with. This meant that the climate changed as well, and both these factors influenced the types of plants that grew. These changes happened slowly over millions of years and animals adapted accordingly. At the beginning of the dinosaur age, low shrubby fern-like plants dominated the landscape. Then came a time when huge coniferous forests and groves of cycads flourished. Later on, the biggest change of all happened when the first flowering plants began to appear. Many plants and flowers that the dinosaurs may have eaten can still be seen growing today.

FIR FEAST
Herbivorous dinosaurs had ample vegetation to satisfy their appetites. Duckbilled dinosaurs, such as *Parasaurolophus*, above, could cope with tough plants because their jaws and teeth were so powerful. Even fir needles posed no problem.

ANCIENT PUZZLE
Living monkey puzzle trees are relatives of ones which flourished long before dinosaurs ever trod the Earth.

CYCAD FROND
Cycads were abundant during most of the dinosaur reign, and are still to be seen today, although they are quite rare.

A DINOSAUR HOME
This scene shows the type of landscape that would have been familiar to dinosaurs of about 130 million years ago. Horsetails, ferns, and cycads abound.

Conifer:
Pseudotsuga menziesii

Passion flower:
Passiflora sp.

Holly:
Ilex aquifolium

Cycad:
Cycas revoluta

THE FLOWERING
The first flowering plant appeared during the last period of the dinosaurs' reign. Flowering plants can reproduce more quickly than other types, and they rapidly came to dominate plant communities worldwide. Flowers changed the diets of dinosaurs dramatically.

A MAGNOLIA
It is surprising to think of dinosaurs eating flowers, but when magnolias appeared about 100 million years ago they were no doubt munched upon by many plant-eating dinosaurs.

Ginkgo:
Ginkgo biloba

Cherry Laurel:
Prunus laurocerasus
"Otto Luykeres"

Magnolia:
Magnolia loebneri

FERN FEEDER
Dinosaurs such as *Stegosaurus* fed on low-growing vegetation like ferns (p. 34). Others, such as the long-necked sauropods, tackled the tougher vegetation of the high conifer forests and cycad groves.

Fern:
Marattia werneri

Fern:
Blechnum sp.

Dogwood:
Cornus alba

Horsetail:
Equisetum giganteum

11

Little and large

A LOT OF PEOPLE think of dinosaurs as being massive creatures, big enough to reach the treetops, but there were also tiny dinosaurs, ones that would not even reach your knee. The biggest creatures ever to walk the Earth were the sauropod group of dinosaurs, which were all plant eaters. *Brachiosaurus* was the biggest sauropod that we know much about. Weighing about 70 tons, it was 22 m (70 ft) long, and stood at 12 m (39 ft) high - about as tall as a four-storey building, or a big oak tree. Bones have recently been found belonging to dinosaurs that may have been even larger than *Brachiosaurus*. Named *Supersaurus* and *Ultrasaurus*, they may have been a third larger than *Brachiosaurus*! When alive, *Ultrasaurus* would have weighed as much as 20 large elephants. By contrast with these quite peaceful giants, the tiny dinosaurs like *Compsognathus* (far right) were mostly agile, crafty meat eaters, some no heavier than a cat.

AS TALL AS A HOUSE
This French engraving shows a popular image of dinosaurs as giants: an alarming visitor to a Paris street investigates a balcony on the fifth floor of a tall building.

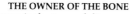

THE OWNER OF THE BONE
This *Brachiosaurus* is the type of dinosaur that owned the massive leg bone (far right). The huge, pillar-like forelimbs were longer than the hindlimbs - probably to help it to reach up to the treetops for food.

FANTASTIC FEMUR
The femur (upper leg bone) shown right belonged to a *Brachiosaurus*. If you stood next to a *Brachiosaurus* leg, you would hardly reach past its knee bone! The gentleman (left) is examining an *Apatosaurus* femur, which measures 2.1 m (6 ft 9 in) long. *Apatosaurus* was another type of sauropod dinosaur.

Part of a large *Brachiosaurus* femur, ending in knee joint

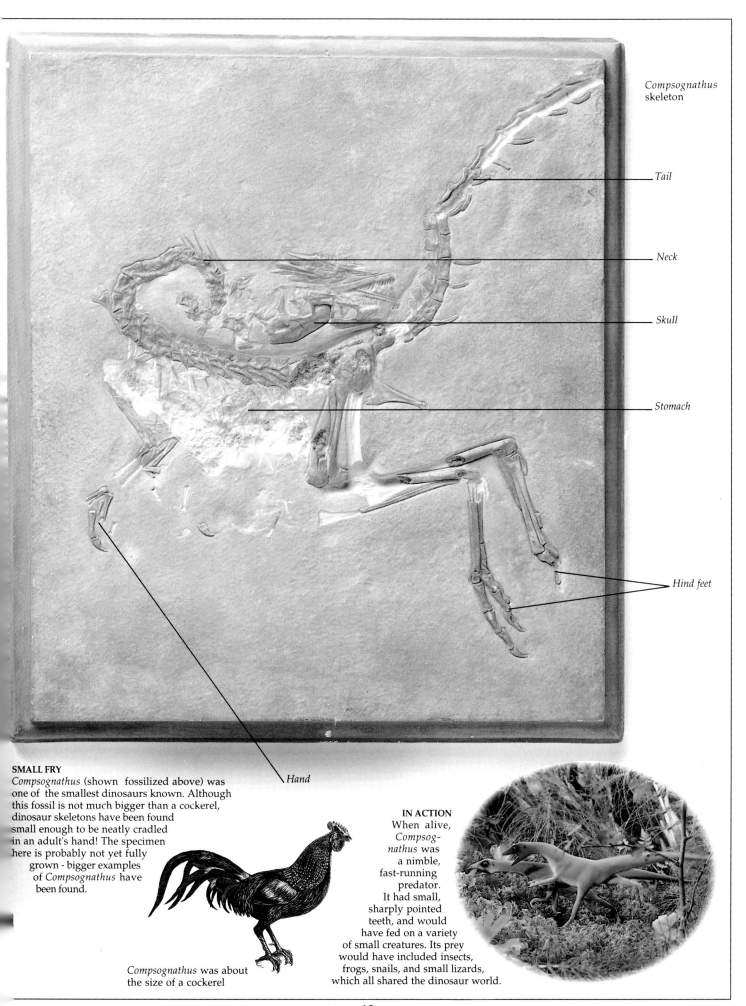

Compsognathus skeleton

Tail

Neck

Skull

Stomach

Hind feet

Hand

SMALL FRY
Compsognathus (shown fossilized above) was one of the smallest dinosaurs known. Although this fossil is not much bigger than a cockerel, dinosaur skeletons have been found small enough to be neatly cradled in an adult's hand! The specimen here is probably not yet fully grown - bigger examples of *Compsognathus* have been found.

Compsognathus was about the size of a cockerel

IN ACTION
When alive, *Compsognathus* was a nimble, fast-running predator. It had small, sharply pointed teeth, and would have fed on a variety of small creatures. Its prey would have included insects, frogs, snails, and small lizards, which all shared the dinosaur world.

The long-necked beast

THE MASSIVE CREATURE that can be seen spread across the next eight pages was one of the biggest dinosaurs ever to walk the Earth. It was called *Diplodocus*, and like *Mamenchisaurus*, opposite, it belonged to a group of dinosaurs called sauropods (p. 12). *Diplodocus* looked extraordinary with its long neck and tail, and a head that was tiny in proportion to the rest of its body. This type of body suited its lifestyle perfectly. It could reach up to feed at the tops of the very tall trees, like conifers, that grew at the time. Its small head allowed it to browse amongst the vegetation, where few other dinosaurs could reach. This type of feeding needed a special type of neck - one that was strong, light, and flexible, in order to be raised and lowered easily. Having stripped one area bare of food, it would have ambled off with its companions in search of new feeding grounds. If *Diplodocus* was threatened by a meat eater, its only defence would have been its bulk, and its long, whip-like tail (pp. 20-21).

Small skull compared to size of body

MAN AND BEAST
When a man is shown next to *Diplodocus*, the enormous size of the skeleton can be appreciated. *Diplodocus* was 26 m (86 ft) long, and its great weight (15 tons) was supported by huge straight legs, like pillars.

Cycad plant would have formed part of Diplodocus' *diet*

SHORT AND FLEXIBLE
Unlike *Diplodocus*, a predator such as *Tyrannosaurus rex* (left) needed a neck that was short, powerful, and flexible. It had to be short to support the large vicious head. Flexibility in the neck meant that *Tyrannosaurus rex* could twist its head around to wrench flesh from its prey.

A HARD NECK
Triceratops' neck (left) needed to be short and extremely strong in order to support the weight of its head. As well as using the force of its head to wrench off tough vegetation, it also fought and charged enemies with its three formidable horns (pp. 30-31).

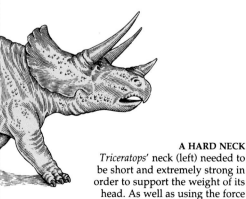

A GIRAFFE'S LIFE
Reaching up with their long necks to the treetops to feed, giraffes are a little like *Diplodocus*. Unlike the dinosaur, however, a giraffe can chew its food, so it does not need such a large belly.

DIPLODOCUS AT HOME
Although *Diplodocus* is often shown living in marshy land, this habitat would not have suited it at all. Because it had quite narrow feet in proportion to its body weight (like an elephant's), it probably would have sunk into the mire and got stuck. It would have preferred a landscape li[ke] this one - dry, with firm ground, where it would browse its way through conifer forests, perhaps as part of a herd.

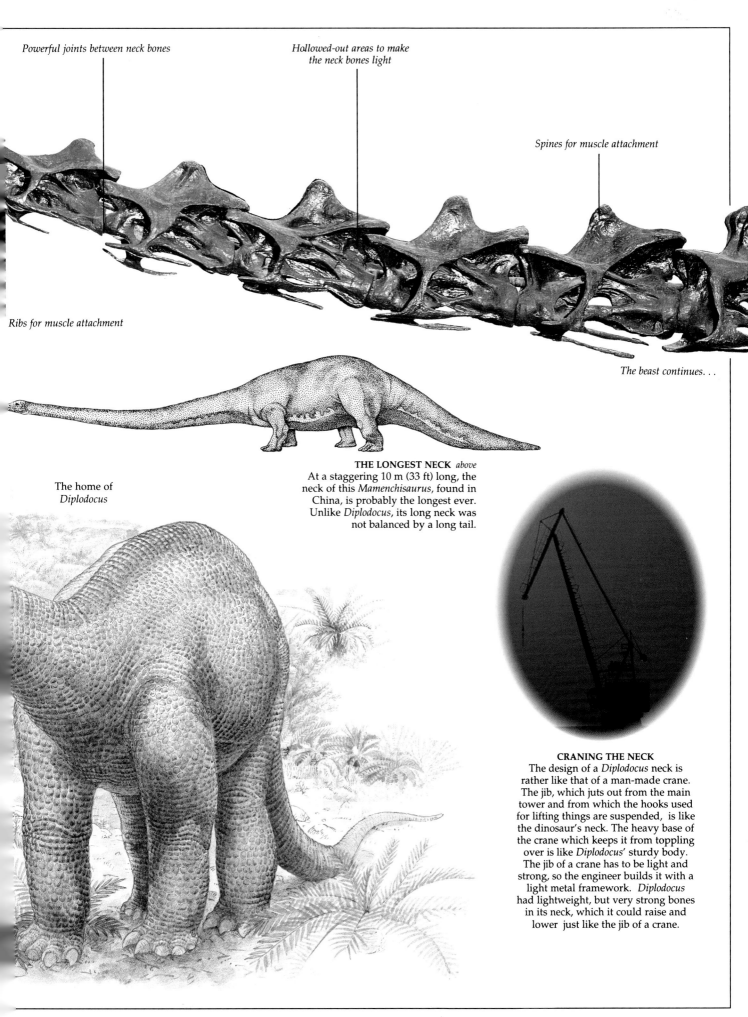

Powerful joints between neck bones

Hollowed-out areas to make the neck bones light

Spines for muscle attachment

Ribs for muscle attachment

The beast continues. . .

THE LONGEST NECK *above*
At a staggering 10 m (33 ft) long, the neck of this *Mamenchisaurus*, found in China, is probably the longest ever. Unlike *Diplodocus*, its long neck was not balanced by a long tail.

The home of
Diplodocus

CRANING THE NECK
The design of a *Diplodocus* neck is rather like that of a man-made crane. The jib, which juts out from the main tower and from which the hooks used for lifting things are suspended, is like the dinosaur's neck. The heavy base of the crane which keeps it from toppling over is like *Diplodocus'* sturdy body. The jib of a crane has to be light and strong, so the engineer builds it with a light metal framework. *Diplodocus* had lightweight, but very strong bones in its neck, which it could raise and lower just like the jib of a crane.

Neck bone

Scapula
(shoulder blade)

The backbone story

The body of *Diplodocus* was designed to bear and move
enormous weight, and the backbone, between shoulders
and hips, was the powerhouse of the whole animal. The backbones had to be strong enough to support the enormous
weight of the neck, tail, and belly. They were also
hollowed out, however, for lightness. Narrow spines,
pointing upwards from the top of the backbone, acted as
anchor points for powerful back muscles. Long ribs pointing
downward curved around the belly, helping to hold the
backbone in position against the great weight of the belly,
and protecting the internal organs of the animal.

Humerus
(upper arm bone)

Ulna
(forearm bone

Temple of Jupiter,
Athens

Radius
(forearm bone)

Wr

Ha

LEGS LIKE PILLARS
The strong legs of *Diplodocus* supported
its body just as the pillars of this Greek
temple support the heavy stone roof.
The limb bones were heavy and dense,
capable of supporting the enormous
weight of the dinosaur.

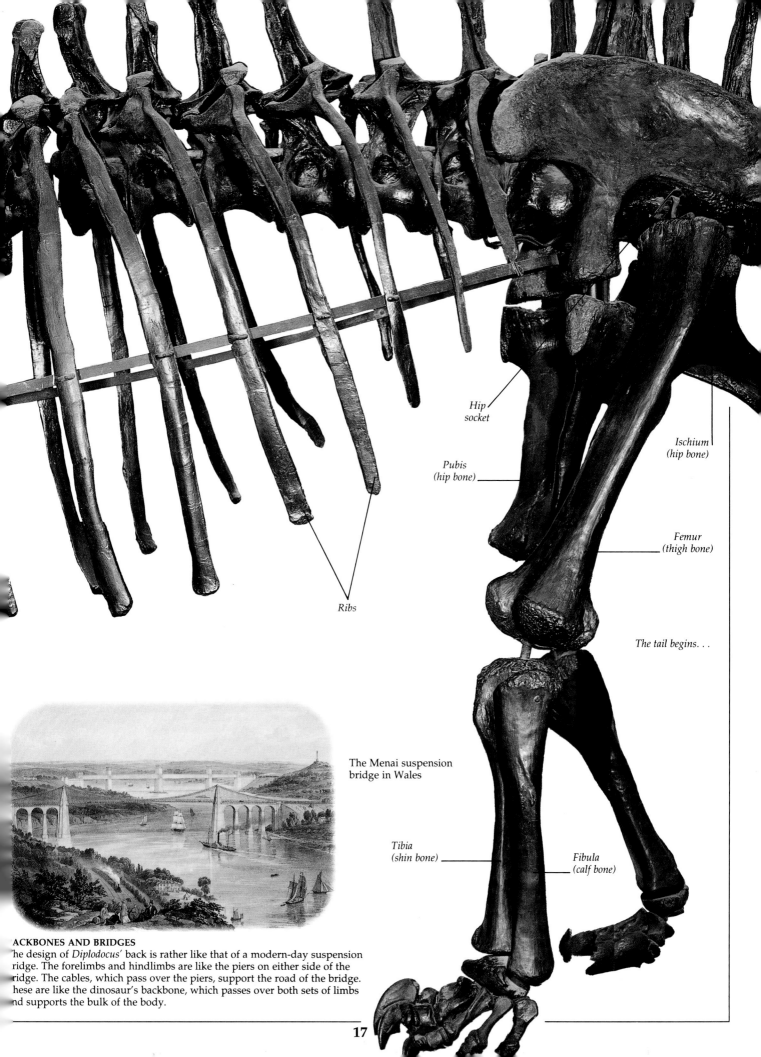

Hip
socket

Ischium
(hip bone)

Pubis
(hip bone)

Femur
(thigh bone)

Ribs

The tail begins. . .

The Menai suspension
bridge in Wales

Tibia
(shin bone)

Fibula
(calf bone)

ACKBONES AND BRIDGES

he design of *Diplodocus'* back is rather like that of a modern-day suspension
ridge. The forelimbs and hindlimbs are like the piers on either side of the
ridge. The cables, which pass over the piers, support the road of the bridge.
hese are like the dinosaur's backbone, which passes over both sets of limbs
nd supports the bulk of the body.

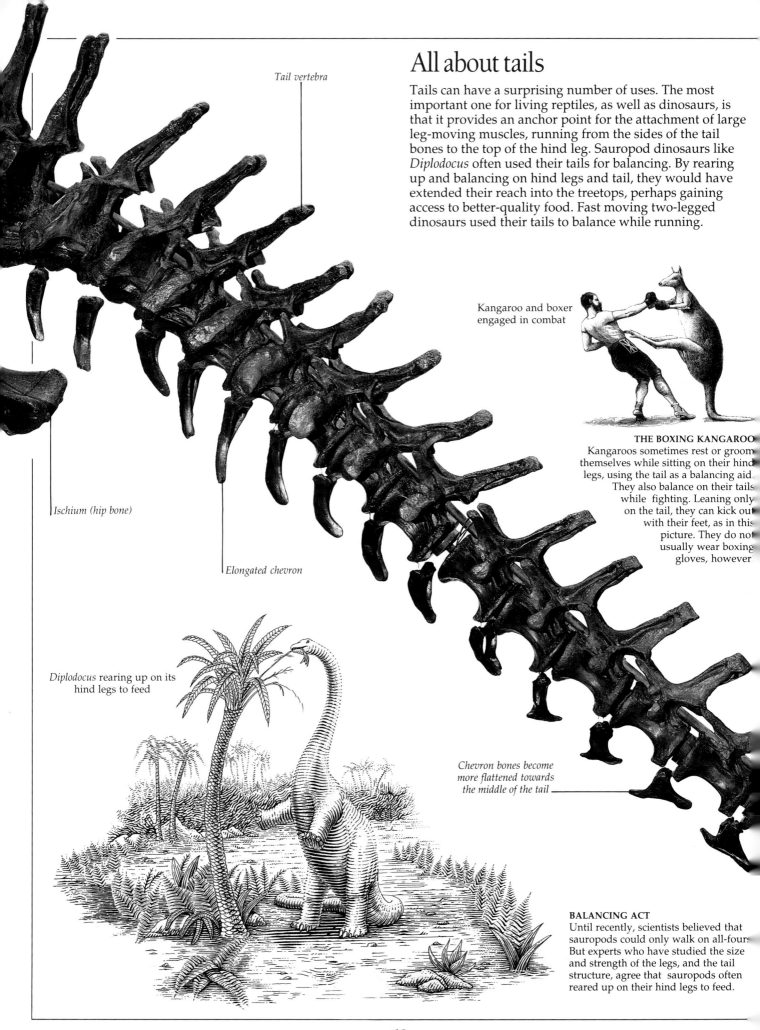

Tail vertebra

All about tails

Tails can have a surprising number of uses. The most important one for living reptiles, as well as dinosaurs, is that it provides an anchor point for the attachment of large leg-moving muscles, running from the sides of the tail bones to the top of the hind leg. Sauropod dinosaurs like *Diplodocus* often used their tails for balancing. By rearing up and balancing on hind legs and tail, they would have extended their reach into the treetops, perhaps gaining access to better-quality food. Fast moving two-legged dinosaurs used their tails to balance while running.

Kangaroo and boxer engaged in combat

THE BOXING KANGAROO
Kangaroos sometimes rest or groom themselves while sitting on their hind legs, using the tail as a balancing aid. They also balance on their tails while fighting. Leaning only on the tail, they can kick out with their feet, as in this picture. They do not usually wear boxing gloves, however

Ischium (hip bone)

Elongated chevron

Diplodocus rearing up on its hind legs to feed

Chevron bones become more flattened towards the middle of the tail

BALANCING ACT
Until recently, scientists believed that sauropods could only walk on all-fours. But experts who have studied the size and strength of the legs, and the tail structure, agree that sauropods often reared up on their hind legs to feed.

18

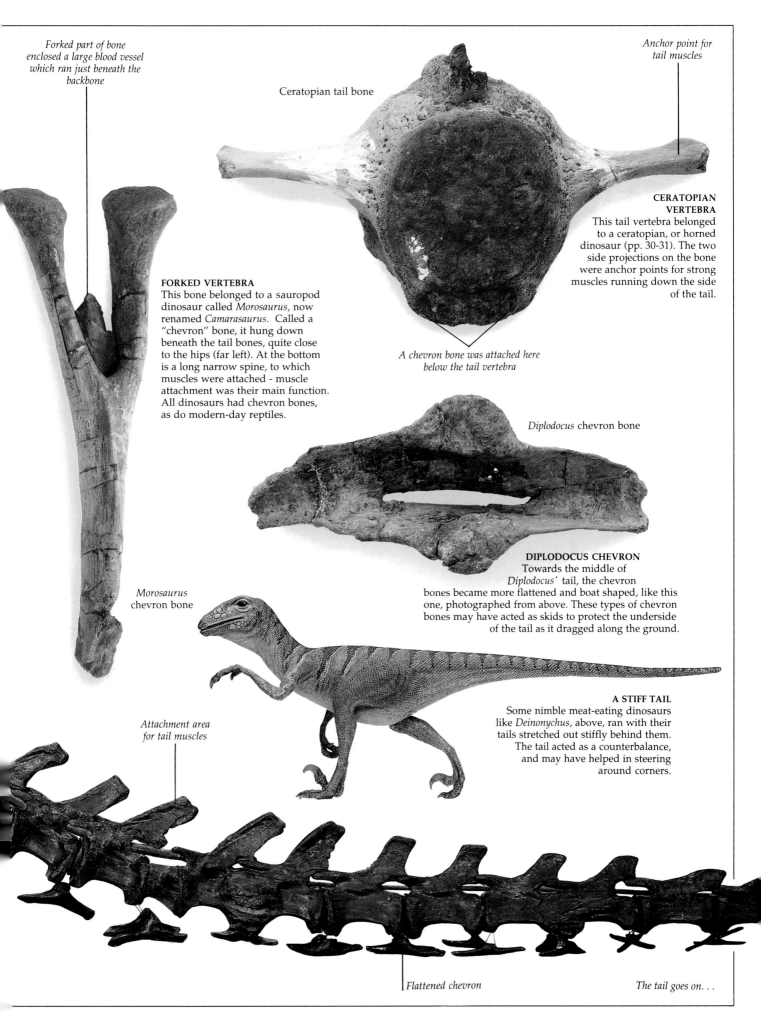

Forked part of bone enclosed a large blood vessel which ran just beneath the backbone

Ceratopian tail bone

Anchor point for tail muscles

CERATOPIAN VERTEBRA
This tail vertebra belonged to a ceratopian, or horned dinosaur (pp. 30-31). The two side projections on the bone were anchor points for strong muscles running down the side of the tail.

FORKED VERTEBRA
This bone belonged to a sauropod dinosaur called *Morosaurus*, now renamed *Camarasaurus*. Called a "chevron" bone, it hung down beneath the tail bones, quite close to the hips (far left). At the bottom is a long narrow spine, to which muscles were attached - muscle attachment was their main function. All dinosaurs had chevron bones, as do modern-day reptiles.

A chevron bone was attached here below the tail vertebra

Diplodocus chevron bone

DIPLODOCUS CHEVRON
Towards the middle of *Diplodocus'* tail, the chevron bones became more flattened and boat shaped, like this one, photographed from above. These types of chevron bones may have acted as skids to protect the underside of the tail as it dragged along the ground.

Morosaurus chevron bone

Attachment area for tail muscles

A STIFF TAIL
Some nimble meat-eating dinosaurs like *Deinonychus*, above, ran with their tails stretched out stiffly behind them. The tail acted as a counterbalance, and may have helped in steering around corners.

Flattened chevron

The tail goes on. . .

The tale of defence

Tails were a very useful means of defence for many plant-eating dinosaurs, and what they lacked in teeth and claws was compensated for by their ingenious tails. Some dinosaurs, like the sauropods, had long, thin tails which they used as whiplashes. Apart from their daunting size, this was their main form of defence. Armoured dinosaurs, or ankylosaurs, had bony clubs on their tails, as well as being protected from head to toe with body armour. Stegosaurs, or plated dinosaurs (pp. 34-35), sported formidable sharp tail spikes which they used to lash out at attackers. Some modern-day reptiles use their tails in self-defence: crocodiles will lash out at an enemy with their heavy, scale-covered tails, and many lizards have long whiplash-type tails. No living reptiles, however, have defensive tails with attachments as spectacular as the formidable spikes and clubs used by some dinosaurs to defend themselves.

A SEVERE BLOW
Shown here delivering a crippling blow to a tyrannosaur is the armoured dinosaur *Euoplocephalus*. Although no match for the meat eater in size, *Euoplocephalus* could topple and disable the tyrannosaur with one well-aimed blow of its tail club.

THORNY DEVIL
Some living reptiles, like this Moloch lizard, are so well armoured from head to toe that they don't need a special defensive tail. Few predators would attempt an attack on this spiky lizard. It lives in dry or desert areas of Australia.

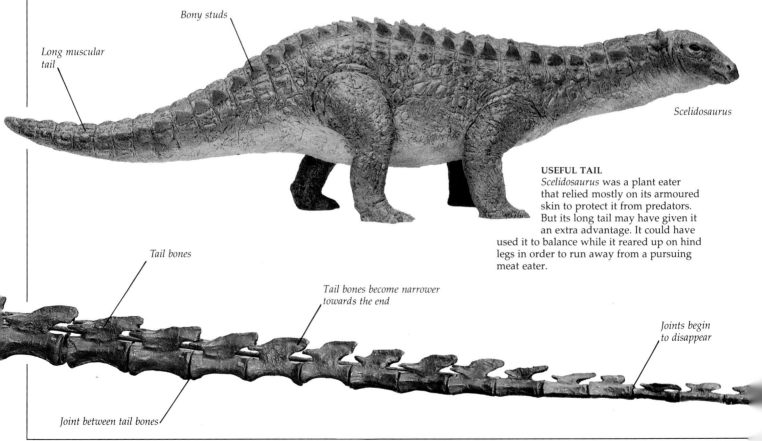

Bony studs

Long muscular tail

Scelidosaurus

USEFUL TAIL
Scelidosaurus was a plant eater that relied mostly on its armoured skin to protect it from predators. But its long tail may have given it an extra advantage. It could have used it to balance while it reared up on hind legs in order to run away from a pursuing meat eater.

Tail bones

Tail bones become narrower towards the end

Joints begin to disappear

Joint between tail bones

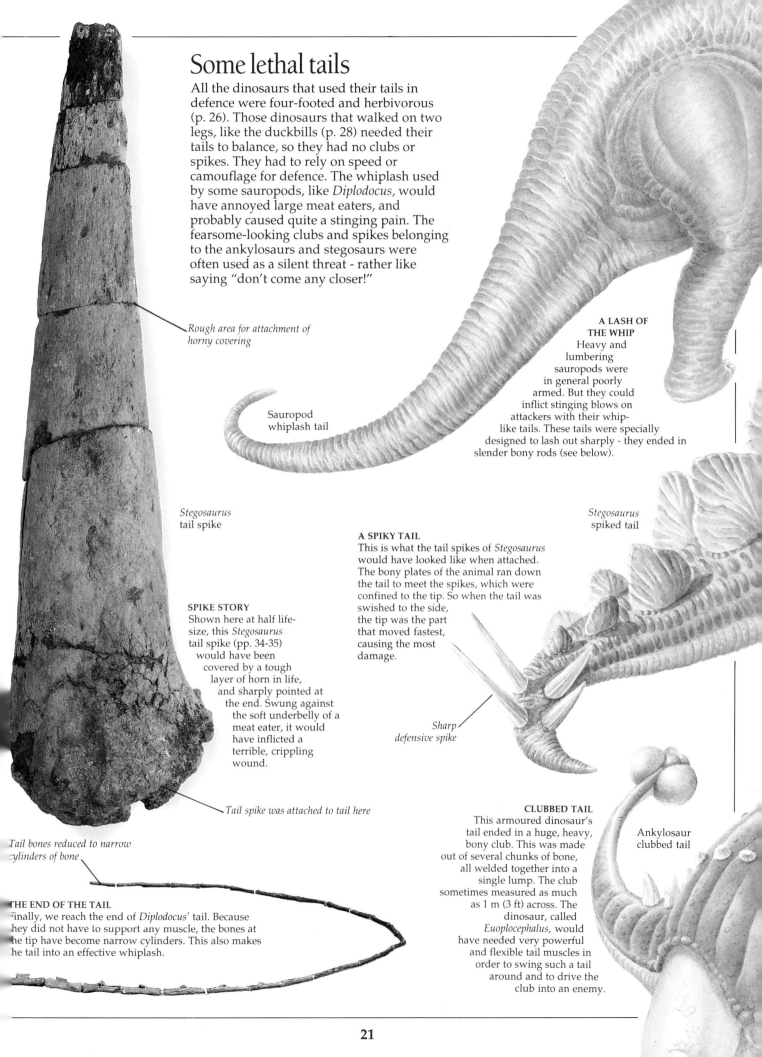

Some lethal tails

All the dinosaurs that used their tails in defence were four-footed and herbivorous (p. 26). Those dinosaurs that walked on two legs, like the duckbills (p. 28) needed their tails to balance, so they had no clubs or spikes. They had to rely on speed or camouflage for defence. The whiplash used by some sauropods, like *Diplodocus*, would have annoyed large meat eaters, and probably caused quite a stinging pain. The fearsome-looking clubs and spikes belonging to the ankylosaurs and stegosaurs were often used as a silent threat - rather like saying "don't come any closer!"

Rough area for attachment of horny covering

Sauropod whiplash tail

A LASH OF THE WHIP
Heavy and lumbering sauropods were in general poorly armed. But they could inflict stinging blows on attackers with their whip-like tails. These tails were specially designed to lash out sharply - they ended in slender bony rods (see below).

Stegosaurus tail spike

Stegosaurus spiked tail

A SPIKY TAIL
This is what the tail spikes of *Stegosaurus* would have looked like when attached. The bony plates of the animal ran down the tail to meet the spikes, which were confined to the tip. So when the tail was swished to the side, the tip was the part that moved fastest, causing the most damage.

SPIKE STORY
Shown here at half life-size, this *Stegosaurus* tail spike (pp. 34-35) would have been covered by a tough layer of horn in life, and sharply pointed at the end. Swung against the soft underbelly of a meat eater, it would have inflicted a terrible, crippling wound.

Sharp defensive spike

Tail spike was attached to tail here

Tail bones reduced to narrow cylinders of bone

THE END OF THE TAIL
Finally, we reach the end of *Diplodocus'* tail. Because they did not have to support any muscle, the bones at the tip have become narrow cylinders. This also makes the tail into an effective whiplash.

CLUBBED TAIL
This armoured dinosaur's tail ended in a huge, heavy, bony club. This was made out of several chunks of bone, all welded together into a single lump. The club sometimes measured as much as 1 m (3 ft) across. The dinosaur, called *Euoplocephalus*, would have needed very powerful and flexible tail muscles in order to swing such a tail around and to drive the club into an enemy.

Ankylosaur clubbed tail

Dinosaur diets

MANY OF US IMAGINE DINOSAURS as being fearsome meat-eating creatures. But some were peaceful plant eaters that simply browsed amongst the treetops, tearing off leaves. Other dinosaurs were able to eat a mixed diet of meat and plants, like humans. Those that were not vegetarian did not confine themselves to dinosaur meat. They would have eaten anything that moved, including insects and birds. Fossilized dinosaur remains can tell us a lot about what the animal ate when it was alive. The most important clues are to be found in the shape and arrangement of the jaws and teeth. Even the overall shape of a dinosaur's body tells a story - meat eaters often had big heads and short, powerful necks in order to wrench lumps of meat off a kill. The long necks of many plant eaters were useful for reaching up to the treetops to feed.

BY THE RIVER
This scene from 190 million years ago shows meat-eating dinosaurs, swimming reptiles, and flying pterosaurs sharing the same landscape.

TIME FOR DINNER?
This scene shows a carnivorous dinosaur rearing over its prey, a well-armoured ankylosaur (pp. 32-33).

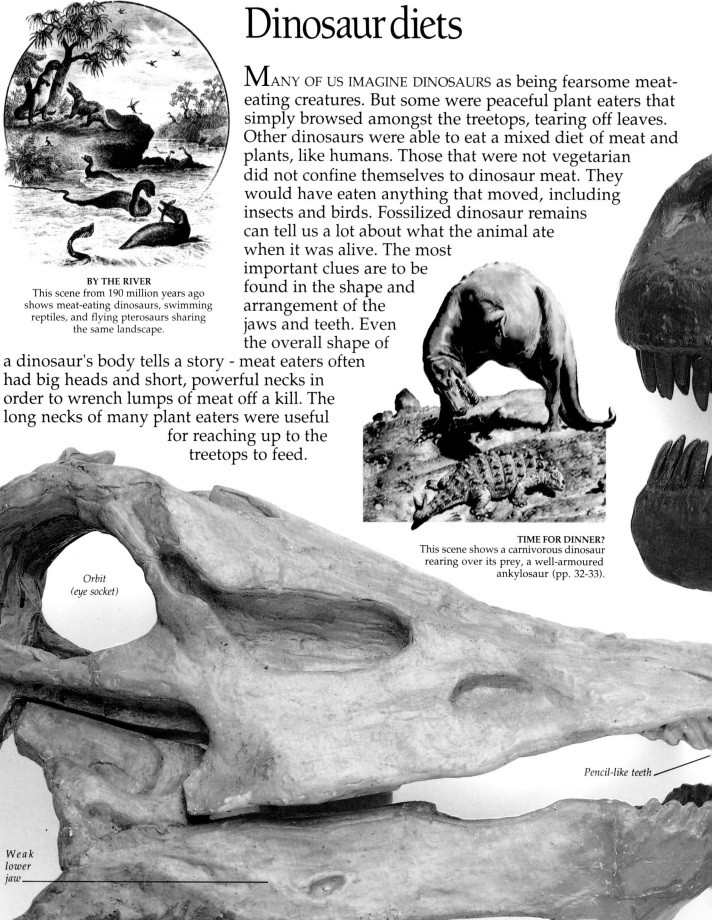

Orbit (eye socket)

Pencil-like teeth

Weak lower jaw

Diplodocus skull

SERIOUS TEETH
The fearsome rows of curved, serrated teeth in the *Allosaurus* skull (below) are typical of carnivores (meat eaters). The "windows" in the massive skull helped to reduce its weight. *Allosaurus* may well have fed on the young of herbivores such as *Diplodocus* (opposite). An adult *Diplodocus* would have been too big to tackle, unless *Allosaurus* hunted in packs.

Large cavity in front of eye for jaw muscles

Orbit (eye socket)

Large serrated teeth

Allosaurus skull

VEGETARIAN SKULL *left*
This skull belonged to a huge plant eater, or herbivore, called *Diplodocus*. All of the thin, pencil-like teeth are at the front of the mouth. *Diplodocus* would have used them like a rake to draw in conifer needles and leaves. Unable to chew, *Diplodocus* simply swallowed what it raked in.

Powerful lower jaw

Diplodocus

Orbit (eye socket)

Massospondylus skull (below)

Small coarse teeth

DIPLODOCUS DINNER
Diplodocus may have raked in plants like this fern leaf. Because it never chewed, it did not need a strong lower jaw.

DUAL DIET DINOSAUR
The skull above belonged to *Massospondylus* . Its teeth, being neither serrated and stabbing, nor rake-like or grinding, were "multi-purpose". Small and coarse-edged, they could chew either meat or plants. Animals who can eat like this are called omnivores.

23

Meat eaters

ALL THE MEAT-EATING DINOSAURS belonged to a group called Theropoda, which literally means "beast footed". Some of the meat-eating dinosaurs were called carnosaurs or "flesh lizards" - large animals with big heads, powerful legs, and short arms. Like all theropods, they walked on two legs, probably not very fast because of the bulk they had to carry. They had big heads to accommodate long jaws which were lined with huge curved teeth, serrated like steak knives. Carnosaurs pursued and ate other dinosaurs, or else fed on corpses that they found. They would kill their prey with the help of their clawed feet and then tear off the flesh of the victim with their hands - well-equipped with sharp claws - and teeth. The other meat eaters were known as coelurosaurs, or "hollow-tailed lizards". By contrast with the carnosaurs, they were lightly built nimble creatures with long grasping arms and hands, and long, narrow jaws. They could run very fast, in order to catch small mammals and insects. After a carnosaur had eaten its fill, a coelurosaur would often move in to eat the scraps that were left.

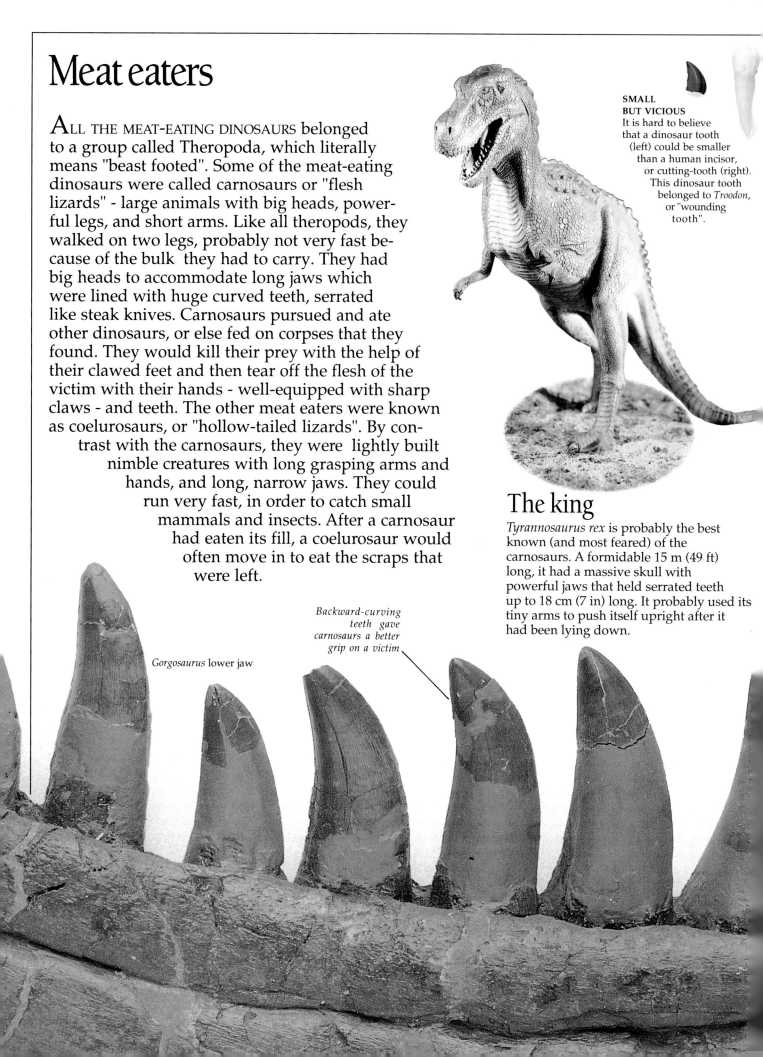

SMALL BUT VICIOUS
It is hard to believe that a dinosaur tooth (left) could be smaller than a human incisor, or cutting-tooth (right). This dinosaur tooth belonged to *Troodon*, or "wounding tooth".

The king

Tyrannosaurus rex is probably the best known (and most feared) of the carnosaurs. A formidable 15 m (49 ft) long, it had a massive skull with powerful jaws that held serrated teeth up to 18 cm (7 in) long. It probably used its tiny arms to push itself upright after it had been lying down.

Gorgosaurus lower jaw

Backward-curving teeth gave carnosaurs a better grip on a victim

NUTHETES TOOTH
Still embedded in rock, this tooth came from a small meat eater called *Nuthetes*.

SMALLER GNASHER
Not all tyrannosaur teeth were huge. This small one is curved, in order to hook into its victim.

LION'S SLICER
Meat-eating animals, like lions, have developed special slicing teeth. No dinosaur had a tooth like this.

NEW GNASHER
Meat-eating dinosaurs' teeth kept growing and were constantly replaced throughout life. This megalosaur tooth is a "new" one.

The large, curved tooth of *Megalosaurus*

Fine serrations like those on a steak knife

Cracks which occurred during fossilization

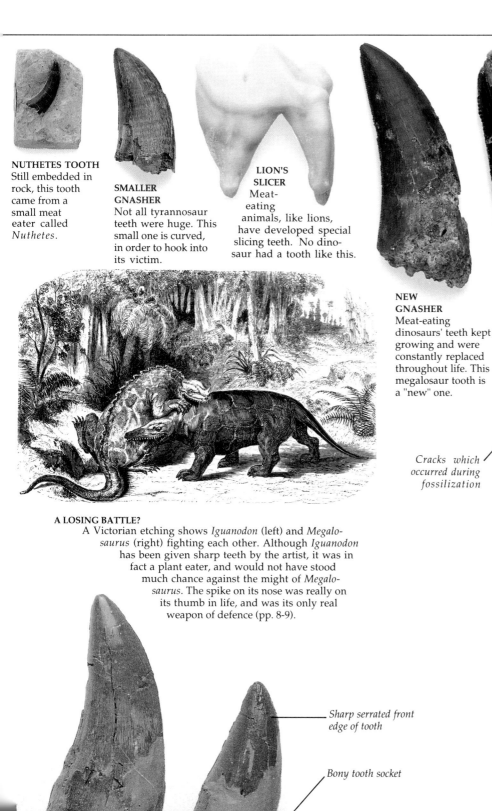

A LOSING BATTLE?
A Victorian etching shows *Iguanodon* (left) and *Megalosaurus* (right) fighting each other. Although *Iguanodon* has been given sharp teeth by the artist, it was in fact a plant eater, and would not have stood much chance against the might of *Megalosaurus*. The spike on its nose was really on its thumb in life, and was its only real weapon of defence (pp. 8-9).

Sharp serrated front edge of tooth

Bony tooth socket

Inner side of jaw bone

THE BIGGEST...
This large *Megalosaurus* tooth is of a typical carnosaur shape, with its curved edge pointing backwards. The edges of the tooth are sharp, with saw-like serrations for cutting meat. The cracks on this specimen appeared during fossilization.

Ceratosaurus skull (below)

LETHAL JAW BONE
This *Gorgosaurus* lower jaw (left) stretched the length of the animal's skull. Powerful jaw muscles, reaching up behind the eye, were attached to the area without teeth. These would have produced a powerful bite, snapping the jaw shut on impact with its prey. The skull above, which belonged to another carnosaur, shows the same basic design.

Plant eaters

MANY OF THE DINOSAURS were plant eaters, including the biggest of all, the sauropods (pp. 12-13). Eating a diet of plants causes animals many more problems than eating meat. Plants are made of tough materials like cellulose and woody lignin, and need to be broken down before digestion can take place in the animal's stomach. Plant-eating dinosaurs coped with their diet in a variety of ways: the sauropods did not chew at all, but simply swallowed raked-in vegetation. This passed directly to the stomach, and was ground up by deliberately swallowed "gizzard stones" (gastroliths), or fermented by bacteria, as in a cow's stomach. The hadrosaurs, or duckbilled dinosaurs, had special teeth which ground and chopped their food before they swallowed it. Ceratopians tackled tough plants with their extra-strong jaws and scissor-like teeth. All of the bird-hipped dinosaurs (p. 6) were plant eaters.

Plant-eating dinosaurs would have eaten conifers such as this yew leaf

TINY TEETH
This jaw came from *Echinodon*, one of the smallest plant-eating dinosaurs. The tiny teeth had spiky edges, like those of an iguana lizard, which eats a mixed diet of plants and meat.

Main jaw bone

Ceratopian beak

SCISSOR TOOTH
This tooth came from a ceratopian dinosaur, like *Triceratops* (below). After tearing off the vegetation with its beak (far left), it would then have sliced it up with its sharp teeth.

Notch for replacement tooth to slot in

Cycad plant

TOUGH AND STRINGY
Some experts believe that ceratopian dinosaurs evolved specially to eat new kinds of tough plants. They would have eaten the leaves of palm-like cycads (left), and maybe even tackled pine cones (above).

Pine cone

BUILT TO CHEW
Dinosaurs like this *Triceratops* (pp. 30-31) ate tough, fibrous plants (above). *Triceratops*, like many ceratopians, had extremely powerful jaws and sharp teeth to help it to cope with its diet.

CROPPING BEAK
A beak like this ceratopian one (p. 30) was ideal for cropping tough plants. The rough grooves and pits mark the place where the horny covering of keratin was attached. The lower, wider part of the bone (called the predentary) fitted tightly against the lower jaw.

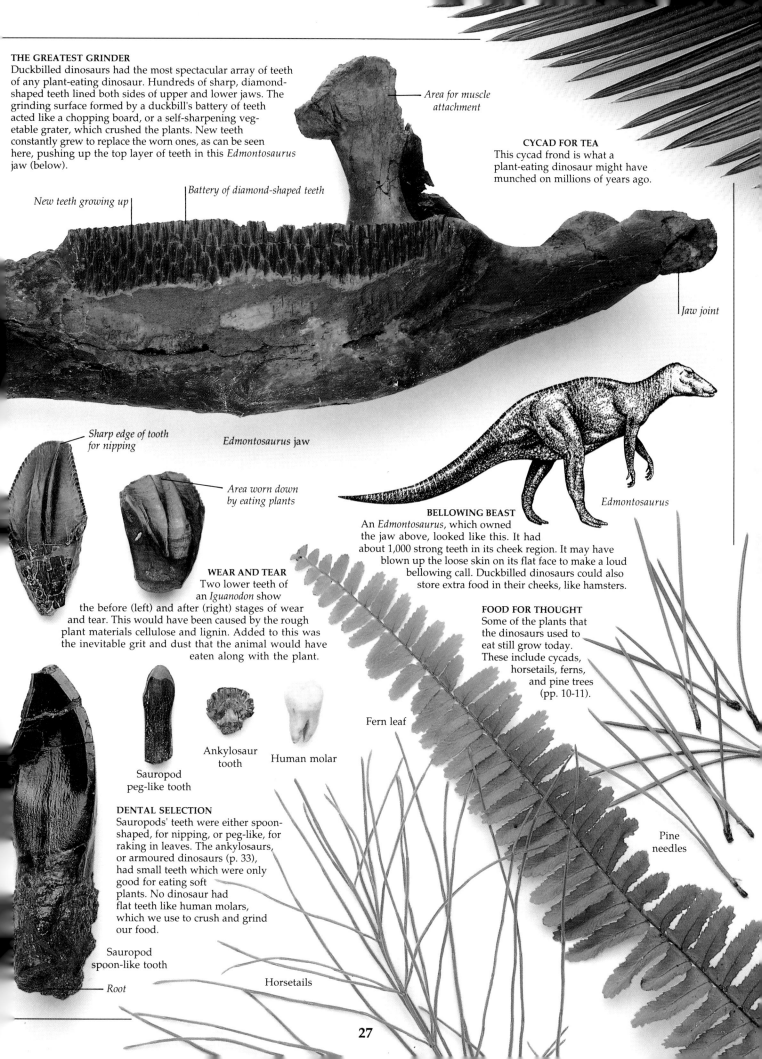

THE GREATEST GRINDER
Duckbilled dinosaurs had the most spectacular array of teeth of any plant-eating dinosaur. Hundreds of sharp, diamond-shaped teeth lined both sides of upper and lower jaws. The grinding surface formed by a duckbill's battery of teeth acted like a chopping board, or a self-sharpening vegetable grater, which crushed the plants. New teeth constantly grew to replace the worn ones, as can be seen here, pushing up the top layer of teeth in this *Edmontosaurus* jaw (below).

Area for muscle attachment

CYCAD FOR TEA
This cycad frond is what a plant-eating dinosaur might have munched on millions of years ago.

New teeth growing up

Battery of diamond-shaped teeth

Jaw joint

Sharp edge of tooth for nipping

Edmontosaurus jaw

Area worn down by eating plants

Edmontosaurus

BELLOWING BEAST
An *Edmontosaurus*, which owned the jaw above, looked like this. It had about 1,000 strong teeth in its cheek region. It may have blown up the loose skin on its flat face to make a loud bellowing call. Duckbilled dinosaurs could also store extra food in their cheeks, like hamsters.

WEAR AND TEAR
Two lower teeth of an *Iguanodon* show the before (left) and after (right) stages of wear and tear. This would have been caused by the rough plant materials cellulose and lignin. Added to this was the inevitable grit and dust that the animal would have eaten along with the plant.

FOOD FOR THOUGHT
Some of the plants that the dinosaurs used to eat still grow today. These include cycads, horsetails, ferns, and pine trees (pp. 10-11).

Fern leaf

Ankylosaur tooth

Human molar

Sauropod peg-like tooth

DENTAL SELECTION
Sauropods' teeth were either spoon-shaped, for nipping, or peg-like, for raking in leaves. The ankylosaurs, or armoured dinosaurs (p. 33), had small teeth which were only good for eating soft plants. No dinosaur had flat teeth like human molars, which we use to crush and grind our food.

Pine needles

Sauropod spoon-like tooth

Root

Horsetails

Peculiar heads

SOME DINOSAURS HAD most oddly shaped heads, sprouting weird and wonderful projections of bone including lumps, bumps, crests, spikes, and helmets. And just as bizarre shapes or brightly coloured patches on reptiles, birds, and even mammals today attract attention, so did the odd shapes of some dinosaurs' heads. They were eye-catching, and could have been used to attract a mate, scare off an enemy, or simply indicate how a dinosaur was feeling - happy or angry! They were often used in attack or defence - a bony head could act like a natural safety-helmet, or a formidable head-butting device. The most spectacular heads belonged to a group of dinosaurs called the hadrosaurs, or duckbills, so-called because of their broad, toothless beaks.

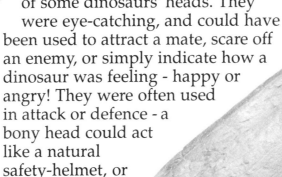

HEAD-CASES
The first two heads in this selection are duckbills: *Parasaurolophus*, with its distinctive long horn, and *Corythosaurus* with its "dinner-plate" shaped crest. The broad, thick head on the right belongs to *Pachycephalosaurus*, one of the "bone-headed" dinosaurs.

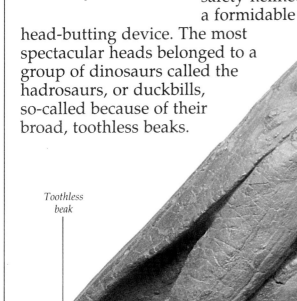

CREST FALLEN?
Different hadrosaurs had different head shapes, but their bodies were all quite similar. Some had heads that were completely unadorned with odd-looking projections, like this one, *Anatosaurus*, one of the most common "crestless" types. It used its broad duck-like beak to scoop up leaves.

Toothless beak

Teeth start here

Parasaurolophus skull

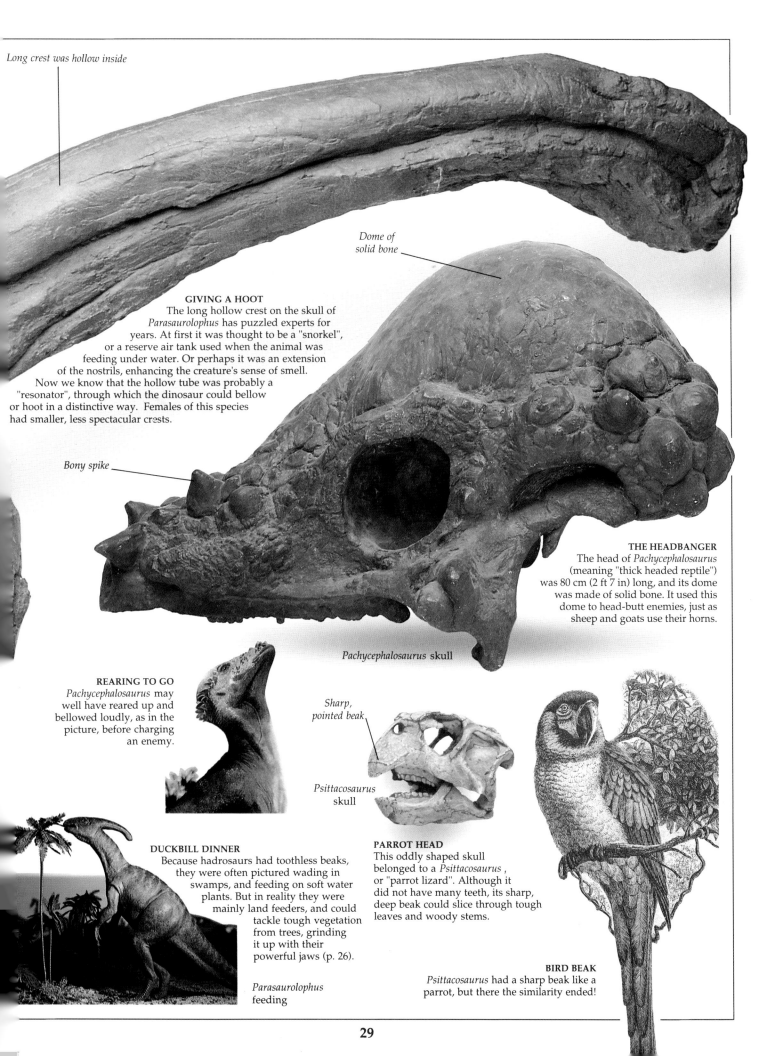

Long crest was hollow inside

Dome of
solid bone

GIVING A HOOT
The long hollow crest on the skull of
Parasaurolophus has puzzled experts for
years. At first it was thought to be a "snorkel",
or a reserve air tank used when the animal was
feeding under water. Or perhaps it was an extension
of the nostrils, enhancing the creature's sense of smell.
Now we know that the hollow tube was probably a
"resonator", through which the dinosaur could bellow
or hoot in a distinctive way. Females of this species
had smaller, less spectacular crests.

Bony spike

THE HEADBANGER
The head of *Pachycephalosaurus*
(meaning "thick headed reptile")
was 80 cm (2 ft 7 in) long, and its
dome was made of solid bone. It used this
dome to head-butt enemies, just as
sheep and goats use their horns.

Pachycephalosaurus skull

REARING TO GO
Pachycephalosaurus may
well have reared up and
bellowed loudly, as in the
picture, before charging
an enemy.

Sharp,
pointed beak

Psittacosaurus
skull

PARROT HEAD
This oddly shaped skull
belonged to a *Psittacosaurus* ,
or "parrot lizard". Although it
did not have many teeth, its sharp,
deep beak could slice through tough
leaves and woody stems.

DUCKBILL DINNER
Because hadrosaurs had toothless beaks,
they were often pictured wading in
swamps, and feeding on soft water
plants. But in reality they were
mainly land feeders, and could
tackle tough vegetation
from trees, grinding
it up with their
powerful jaws (p. 26).

Parasaurolophus
feeding

BIRD BEAK
Psittacosaurus had a sharp beak like a
parrot, but there the similarity ended!

Three-horned face

TRICERATOPS, WHICH MEANS "three-horned face", belonged to a group of dinosaurs known as ceratopians, or horned dinosaurs. Each ceratopian had a large bony frill pointing backwards from the skull and masking the neck, horns on the nose or over the eyes, and a narrow, hooked beak. Most were four-legged and stocky, like the rhinoceroses of today, and all were plant eaters. Many fossils of ceratopians found in the same area suggest that they roamed in herds, confronting a threatening meat eater as a pack. As the ceratopians evolved, their headgear gradually became more pronounced. *Triceratops*, the "king" of the ceratopians, lived at the end of the reign of the dinosaurs, and had the most spectacular array of horns and frills of all the ceratopians: its head took up nearly one-third of its length. With head lowered and the horns pointing forward, all backed up by its enormous bulk, *Triceratops* must have provided a formidable defence to predators such as *Tyrannosaurus rex* (p. 24).

Brow horn

LIKE A RHINO
This model reconstruction of *Triceratops*, based on the study of complete skeletons of the animal, is probably very close to life. Here, the resemblance to modern rhinoceroses is very striking.

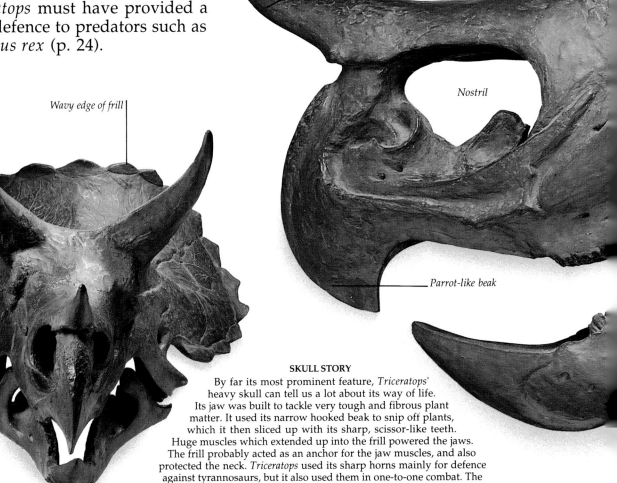

Nose horn

Nostril

Wavy edge of frill

Parrot-like beak

Triceratops
skull - front view

SKULL STORY
By far its most prominent feature, *Triceratops'* heavy skull can tell us a lot about its way of life. Its jaw was built to tackle very tough and fibrous plant matter. It used its narrow hooked beak to snip off plants, which it then sliced up with its sharp, scissor-like teeth. Huge muscles which extended up into the frill powered the jaws. The frill probably acted as an anchor for the jaw muscles, and also protected the neck. *Triceratops* used its sharp horns mainly for defence against tyrannosaurs, but it also used them in one-to-one combat. The male *Triceratops* would lock horns with a member of its own kind and head-wrestle, much as deer, antelope, and sheep do today.

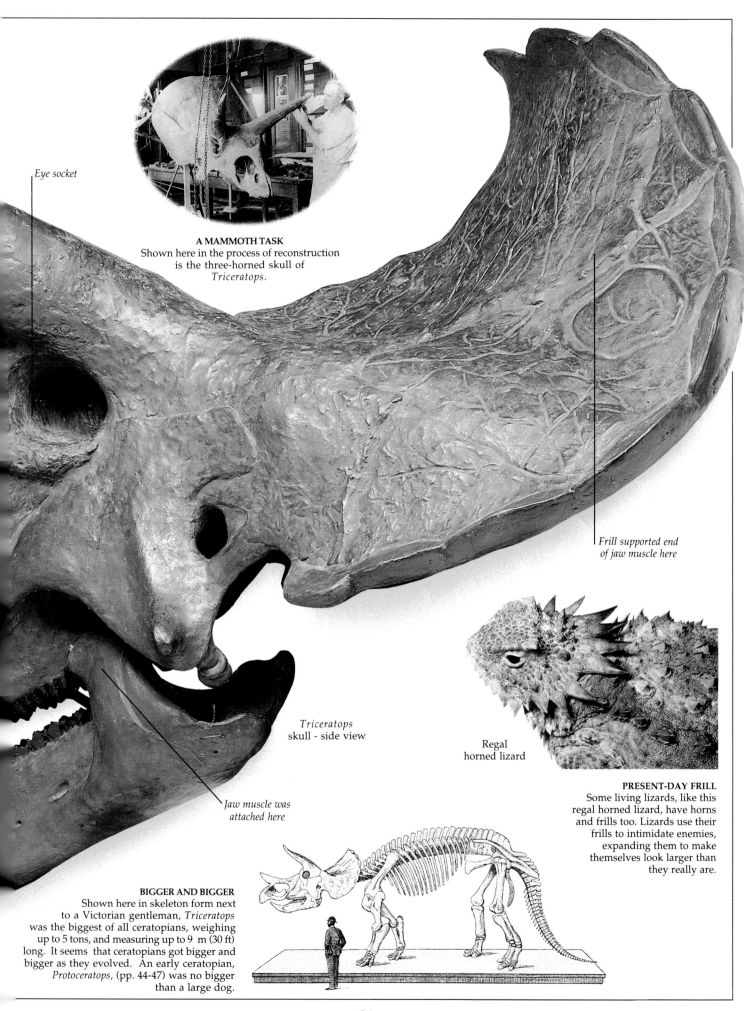

Eye socket

A MAMMOTH TASK
Shown here in the process of reconstruction
is the three-horned skull of
Triceratops.

*Frill supported end
of jaw muscle here*

Triceratops
skull - side view

Regal
horned lizard

*Jaw muscle was
attached here*

PRESENT-DAY FRILL
Some living lizards, like this
regal horned lizard, have horns
and frills too. Lizards use their
frills to intimidate enemies,
expanding them to make
themselves look larger than
they really are.

BIGGER AND BIGGER
Shown here in skeleton form next
to a Victorian gentleman, *Triceratops*
was the biggest of all ceratopians, weighing
up to 5 tons, and measuring up to 9 m (30 ft)
long. It seems that ceratopians got bigger and
bigger as they evolved. An early ceratopian,
Protoceratops, (pp. 44-47) was no bigger
than a large dog.

A tough skin

WHAT WAS dinosaur skin like? Fossilized skin impressions can tell us that it was scaly, like reptile skin, and in some cases armour-plated for extra protection. Dinosaur skin was perfectly suited to life on land. Just like reptile skin, it was waterproof, tough, and horny. Waterproof skin prevents an animal from drying out quickly in air, sun, or wind - animals like frogs have to stay in moist conditions because their skin is thin and not waterproof. Tough, scaly skin protects an animal while it moves about on land, dragging the body over, or between, rough stones, or falling over. Dinosaur skin impressions, like the ones shown here, are usually small, because after death, animal skin rots away too quickly to be fossilized. However, in a few rare cases, an almost entire body impression has been preserved. The dinosaurs that left these impressions probably died in a dry area so that their skin became dried out, before being buried by wind-blown sand. The sand then turned into sand-stone over the years, and was so tightly packed against the skin that when the skin disappeared, its exact shape and pattern remained in the stone. No one knows for sure what colour dinosaur skin was, or whether it had stripes or spots - dinosaurs are most often shown in "muddy" shades of green and brown.

ARMOUR-PLATED MAMMAL
Well protected by its bony armour, the armadillo that lives today is like the ankylosaurs, or armoured dinosaurs (right). They, too, stayed still on the ground while predators were threatening. Few attackers would have been able to get a grip on their tough bodies.

COLOUR CO-ORDINATED
Dinosaurs may well have had brightly coloured skin like this agamid lizard. Skin colour can be useful as camouflage, or as a warning signal. This lizard probably uses his bright-green skin to mark out a territory, or to attract a mate.

SOLITARY NODULE
Bony nodules like this one were mixed in with the overlapping plates on *Polacanthus* skin. These nodules "floated" in the skin beneath the scales, as in living reptiles.

Polacanthus skin impression

A KNOBBLY COAT
This knobbly skin impression came from an armoured dinosaur called *Polacanthus*. Short-legged and squat, it was about 4 m (13 ft) long, and had sharp spines running along its back. These, combined with its overlapping bony plates, would have discouraged hungry meat eaters from attacking.

Raised nodules for protection

LIKE A CROCODILE?
Crocodiles, being reptiles, have the same type of skin as the dinosaurs - ideally adapted to conditions on dry land. The knobbly skin on this "smiling" crocodile is like the *Polacanthus* impression (left).

Central ridge of nodule

ALL ABOUT ANKYLOSAURS

The ankylosaurs had bones which were fused together to form a bony armour. The armoured "tanks" of the dinosaur world, these creatures were squat and very heavy. They looked rather like giant reptilian armadillos. They had small jaws and weak teeth, and ate plants. They protected themselves from large carnivores mainly by crouching and clinging to the ground, relying completely on their tough skins for defence.

THE COMPLETE BEAST

A typical ankylosaur probably looked like this when it was alive. As well as having spikes and nodules, some of these dinosaurs had formidable tail clubs (pp. 20-21) which they swung at the legs of attackers.

Smaller scales for flexibility

ANKYLOSAUR NODULE

Many ankylosaur nodules looked like this one. The flattened base was attached to the creature's back, and the broad central ridge provided protection. In life, it was covered by a horny scale (like a fingernail). In the picture, it is possible to make out the pitted areas where this was attached.

Sauropod skin impression

Bigger scales where skin did not have to bend

UNARMOURED AND SCALY

Quite smooth compared to the ankylosaurs, this skin impression came from a sauropod dinosaur, probably one like *Diplodocus* (pp. 20-21). The skin was scaly, not bony like the ankylosaurs, and would have given little protection against attack. The scales, although packed tightly together, had flexible edges where they touched, acting like "hinges" to allow easy movement. You can see from this impression that the scales varied in size, the smaller ones occurring where the skin had to bend a lot.

Plated dinosaurs

ONE OF THE MOST UNUSUAL GROUPS of dinosaurs were the stegosaurs, named after the North American dinosaur, *Stegosaurus*. Easily recognized by the double row of plates running down their backs, stegosaurs also had sharp spikes on the ends of their tails, used for lashing out in defence. Despite their fearsome appearance, these dinosaurs were all plant eaters. They usually walked on all-fours, browsing on low vegetation - a way of feeding which suited their low-slung heads perfectly. Their small weak teeth could only handle soft plants. The word "stegosaur" actually means "roof lizard", because it was once thought that the plates lay flat on the dinosaur's back, like tiles on a roof. Although this arrangement would have provided slightly better protection against attack from carnosaurs, it is more likely that the plates stood upright in two rows along the stegosaur's back. Some people think that the plates were fixed to the skeleton, but they were actually embedded in the dinosaur's thick skin.

CAUGHT IN THE RAIN
Stegosaurus, shown here caught in a downpour, is most often seen with its plates in two parallel rows down its back. The plates were made of bone with honeycomb-like spaces running through - not much use as defensive armour plating.

A WEIRD STEGOSAUR
This etching shows an early attempt to reconstruct a plated dinosaur - with hedgehog-like spines instead of bony plates! It is unlikely that stegosaurs would have walked on two legs - their front feet were not adapted for any function except walking.

Vertebral spine

Cone-shaped plate

Chevron bone

A STING IN THE TAIL
The large, cone-shaped plates on the back of *Tuojiangosaurus* give way to two pairs of sharply pointed ones, which were used as lethal weapons. Stegosaurs could swing their muscular tails from side to side with great force.

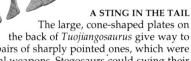

Sharp defensive spike

Broad, fla feet

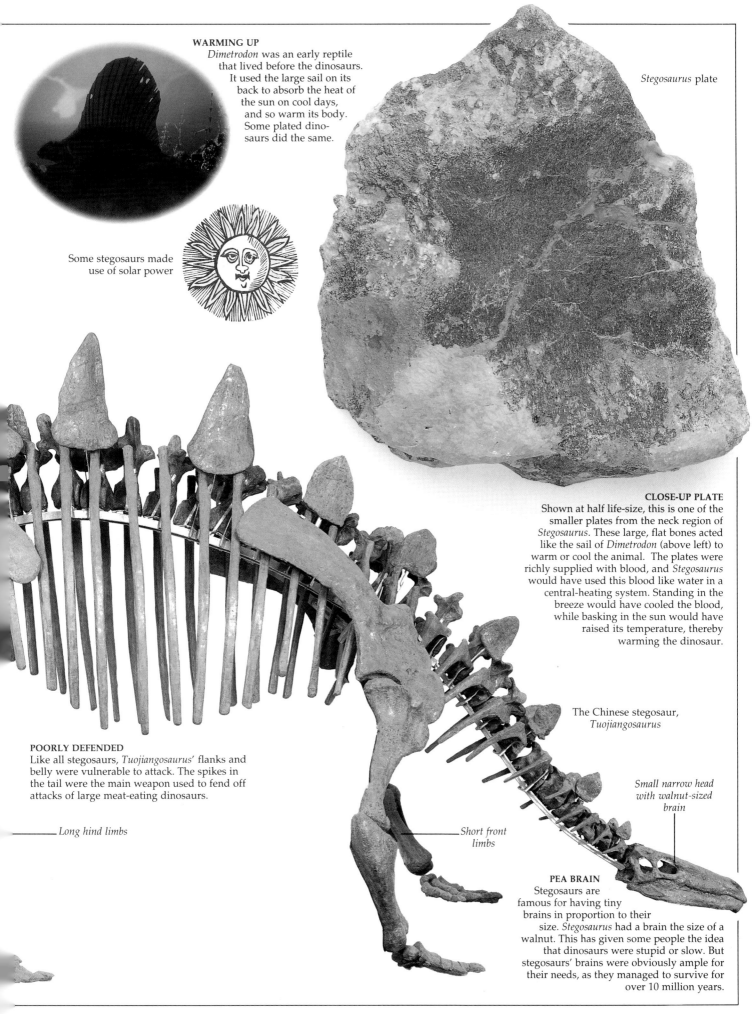

WARMING UP
Dimetrodon was an early reptile that lived before the dinosaurs. It used the large sail on its back to absorb the heat of the sun on cool days, and so warm its body. Some plated dinosaurs did the same.

Some stegosaurs made use of solar power

Stegosaurus plate

CLOSE-UP PLATE
Shown at half life-size, this is one of the smaller plates from the neck region of *Stegosaurus*. These large, flat bones acted like the sail of *Dimetrodon* (above left) to warm or cool the animal. The plates were richly supplied with blood, and *Stegosaurus* would have used this blood like water in a central-heating system. Standing in the breeze would have cooled the blood, while basking in the sun would have raised its temperature, thereby warming the dinosaur.

The Chinese stegosaur, *Tuojiangosaurus*

Small narrow head with walnut-sized brain

POORLY DEFENDED
Like all stegosaurs, *Tuojiangosaurus'* flanks and belly were vulnerable to attack. The spikes in the tail were the main weapon used to fend off attacks of large meat-eating dinosaurs.

Long hind limbs

Short front limbs

PEA BRAIN
Stegosaurs are famous for having tiny brains in proportion to their size. *Stegosaurus* had a brain the size of a walnut. This has given some people the idea that dinosaurs were stupid or slow. But stegosaurs' brains were obviously ample for their needs, as they managed to survive for over 10 million years.

Fast movers

NOT ALL DINOSAURS WERE HUGE and lumbering. Some were built for speed, either to flee attackers, or to pursue prey. Unlike fast-running living animals like horses, which are all four-footed, fast-moving dinosaurs ran on their hind legs alone. As a result, all the fast movers looked quite similar. They all tended to have long back legs, in order to take long strides. Slender legs and narrow feet can be moved quickly and so allowed the dinosaurs to run more efficiently. The rest of the body was usually light and fairly short, balanced by a slender tail. The arms were lightly built, with small-clawed hands, and the neck was long, with a small head on the top. Some of the nimble dinosaurs could reach speeds of 56 kph (35 mph) - almost as fast as a racehorse. They could take advantage of their speed in two ways: either to pursue a victim, or to beat a hasty retreat from an attacker. Herbivorous and carnivorous fast-moving dinosaurs were involved in a kind of "race": plant eaters evolved faster and faster types in order to avoid being caught by ever-improving meat eaters.

OSTRICH LOOKALIKE
Struthiomimus, or ostrich mimic, looked remarkably like an ostrich, and probably ran in a very similar way. The main difference is *Struthiomimus'* long bony tail, and its clawed hands in place of an ostrich's feathered wings.

TINY AND TOOTHY
This fast-moving dinosaur, *Heterodontosaurus*, was only about 1 m (3 ft) long. It had three different types of teeth, but was still a herbivore.

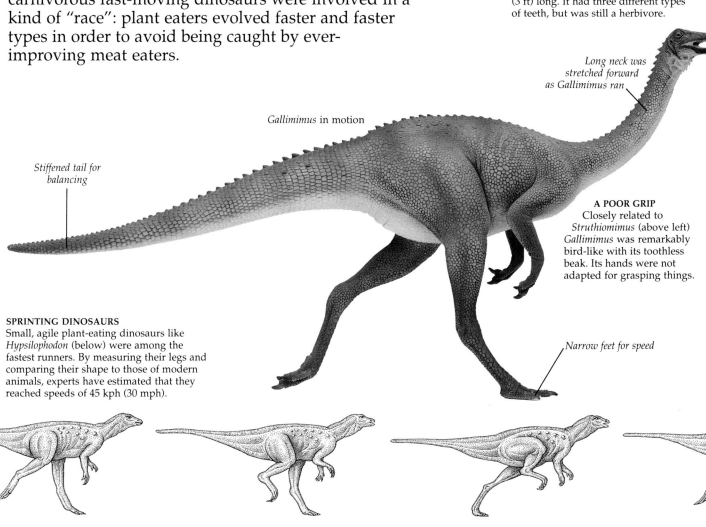

Long neck was stretched forward as Gallimimus ran

Gallimimus in motion

Stiffened tail for balancing

A POOR GRIP
Closely related to *Struthiomimus* (above left) *Gallimimus* was remarkably bird-like with its toothless beak. Its hands were not adapted for grasping things.

SPRINTING DINOSAURS
Small, agile plant-eating dinosaurs like *Hypsilophodon* (below) were among the fastest runners. By measuring their legs and comparing their shape to those of modern animals, experts have estimated that they reached speeds of 45 kph (30 mph).

Narrow feet for speed

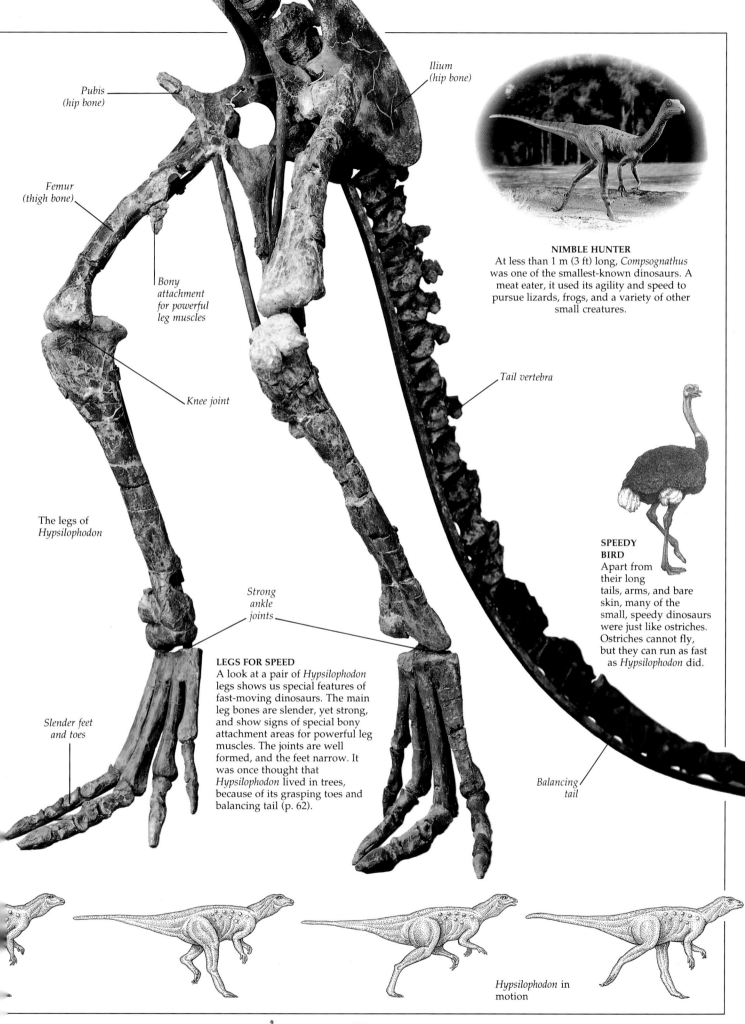

Pubis
(hip bone)

Ilium
(hip bone)

Femur
(thigh bone)

Bony
attachment
for powerful
leg muscles

Knee joint

Tail vertebra

NIMBLE HUNTER
At less than 1 m (3 ft) long, *Compsognathus*
was one of the smallest-known dinosaurs. A
meat eater, it used its agility and speed to
pursue lizards, frogs, and a variety of other
small creatures.

**SPEEDY
BIRD**
Apart from
their long
tails, arms, and bare
skin, many of the
small, speedy dinosaurs
were just like ostriches.
Ostriches cannot fly,
but they can run as fast
as *Hypsilophodon* did.

The legs of
Hypsilophodon

Strong
ankle
joints

LEGS FOR SPEED
A look at a pair of *Hypsilophodon*
legs shows us special features of
fast-moving dinosaurs. The main
leg bones are slender, yet strong,
and show signs of special bony
attachment areas for powerful leg
muscles. The joints are well
formed, and the feet narrow. It
was once thought that
Hypsilophodon lived in trees,
because of its grasping toes and
balancing tail (p. 62).

Slender feet
and toes

Balancing
tail

Hypsilophodon in
motion

Two feet or four?

Why did some dinosaurs walk on four legs, and some on two? The answer is simply that dinosaurs walked in the way that suited their lifestyle best. Most carnivores, for instance, walked on their hind legs, because they needed to use their hands to catch and hold on to their prey. Other dinosaurs walked on all four legs, mainly because their enormous size and weight needed support from four "posts" underneath - many of the large herbivores such as *Diplodocus* (p. 14) were like this. Some dinosaurs had the option of walking either on two or four legs, depending on what they were doing at the time. They could move around slowly on all-fours, feeding on low vegetation, but when alarmed, could rear up and charge off on hind legs alone. These dinosaurs needed special "hands" that allowed for weight support, as well as grasping.

ON TWO LEGS ...
Corythosaurus, a hadrosaur (p. 28) most often adopted this pose, resting or walking on its hind legs. This left its smaller hands free to hold on to plants. *Corythosaurus* probably ran on its hind legs to escape predators like *Tyrannosaurus rex* (far right).

Hoof-like claw

Scelidosaurus foot

... AND ON FOUR
An examination of the hand bones of *Corythosaurus* reveals that several of the fingers ended in broad, flattened hooves (right). These sorts of bones are typical of toes used for walking on, so *Corythosaurus* must have walked on all-fours sometimes.

TOE END
This hadrosaur toe bone from the "hand" is typically flattened and hoof-like.

Hadrosaur toe

Triceratops toe

Ankle bones

FOUR-LEGGED TOE
Triceratops always walked on four legs, so this *Triceratops* toe bone could come from either the front or back foot. The toe bone is broader and more hoof-like than the hadrosaur one (above), which did not use its front feet so much.

SOMETHING AFOOT?
This is the complete hind foot of an early plant-eating dinosaur called *Scelidosaurus*. It was heavily armoured with bony, jaw-breaking studs which ran the length of its body. *Scelidosaurus* always walked on four legs, and its hind foot was strong and broad, with four powerful toes to support the heavy body. The small first toe would have barely reached the ground.

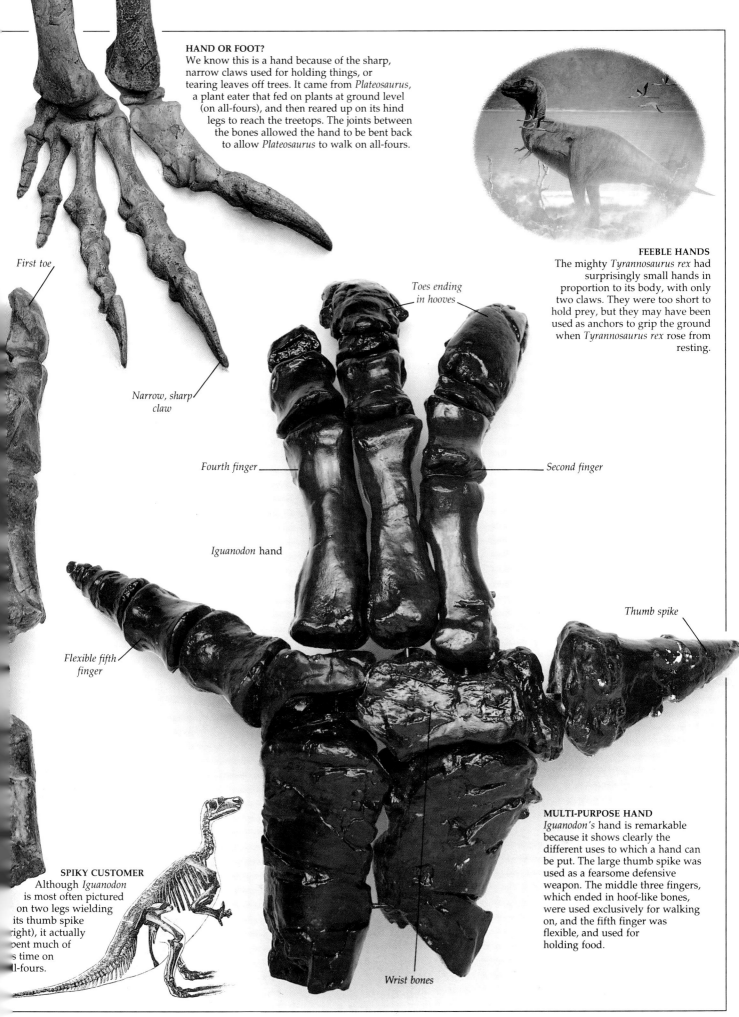

HAND OR FOOT?
We know this is a hand because of the sharp, narrow claws used for holding things, or tearing leaves off trees. It came from *Plateosaurus*, a plant eater that fed on plants at ground level (on all-fours), and then reared up on its hind legs to reach the treetops. The joints between the bones allowed the hand to be bent back to allow *Plateosaurus* to walk on all-fours.

First toe

Narrow, sharp claw

FEEBLE HANDS
The mighty *Tyrannosaurus rex* had surprisingly small hands in proportion to its body, with only two claws. They were too short to hold prey, but they may have been used as anchors to grip the ground when *Tyrannosaurus rex* rose from resting.

Toes ending in hooves

Fourth finger

Second finger

Iguanodon hand

Thumb spike

Flexible fifth finger

SPIKY CUSTOMER
Although *Iguanodon* is most often pictured on two legs wielding its thumb spike (right), it actually spent much of its time on all-fours.

MULTI-PURPOSE HAND
Iguanodon's hand is remarkable because it shows clearly the different uses to which a hand can be put. The large thumb spike was used as a fearsome defensive weapon. The middle three fingers, which ended in hoof-like bones, were used exclusively for walking on, and the fifth finger was flexible, and used for holding food.

Wrist bones

Ancient footprints

THE OWNER
OF THE PRINT
The huge footprint
(right) was made by an
Iguanodon (pp. 8-9).
This plant eater had
small hooves on
both its hands
and feet. It
could walk
on two or
four feet.

AS WELL AS LEAVING their fossilized bones as evidence, dinosaurs also made their mark on the Earth in the form of footprints. Tracks have been found where dinosaurs walked in soft, swampy land, like riverbanks, in search of food and water. Later on, the prints would have dried and hardened in the sun. Eventually, through rain or flooding, water would have brought more sand or mud which buried the prints until they gradually fossilized. Called trace fossils, because they are not actually a part of an animal, these footprints can tell us much about how dinosaurs moved. A lot of the same types of prints found together, for instance, with smaller ones in the middle, suggests that some dinosaurs moved in herds, with the young ones protected in the centre.

**RUNNING ALL
OVER THE WORLD**
Dinosaur trackways have been found all over the world. These tracks found in Queensland, Australia, came from small meat eaters, running together as a pack. Experts can judge the speed at which they were moving by measuring the distance between the prints.

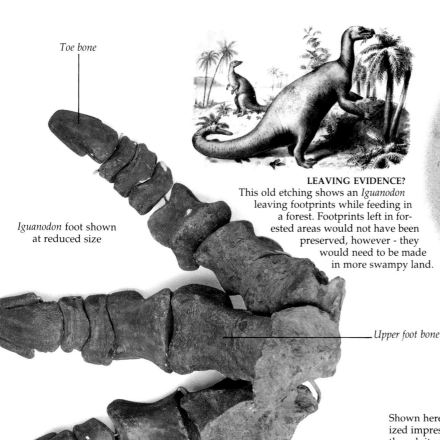

Toe bone

Iguanodon foot shown at reduced size

Upper foot bone

LEAVING EVIDENCE?
This old etching shows an *Iguanodon* leaving footprints while feeding in a forest. Footprints left in forested areas would not have been preserved, however - they would need to be made in more swampy land.

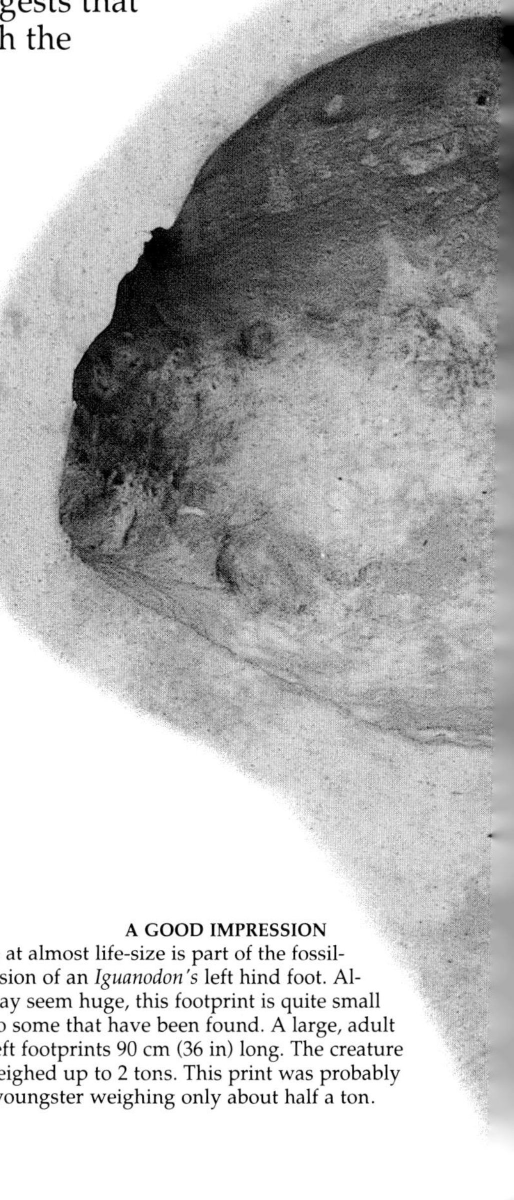

A GOOD IMPRESSION
Shown here at almost life-size is part of the fossilized impression of an *Iguanodon's* left hind foot. Although it may seem huge, this footprint is quite small compared to some that have been found. A large, adult *Iguanodon* left footprints 90 cm (36 in) long. The creature probably weighed up to 2 tons. This print was probably made by a youngster weighing only about half a ton.

FOSSIL FOOT
The three-toed right foot of *Iguanodon* (above) had to be very strong to support the great weight of the animal. *Iguanodon* probably walked on its toes, like cats and dogs do today. The foot leaves a clover-leaf shaped footprint, many of which have been found in southern Britain. The heavier the dinosaur, the better the footprint (right).

Iguanodon footprint

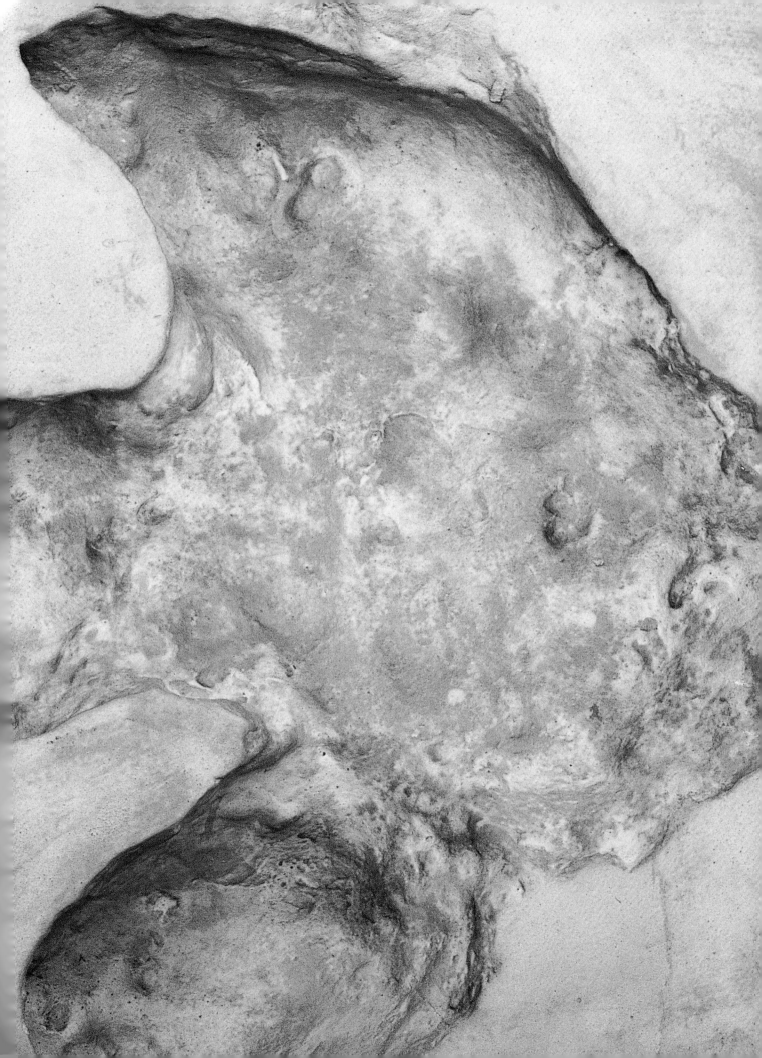

Claws and their uses

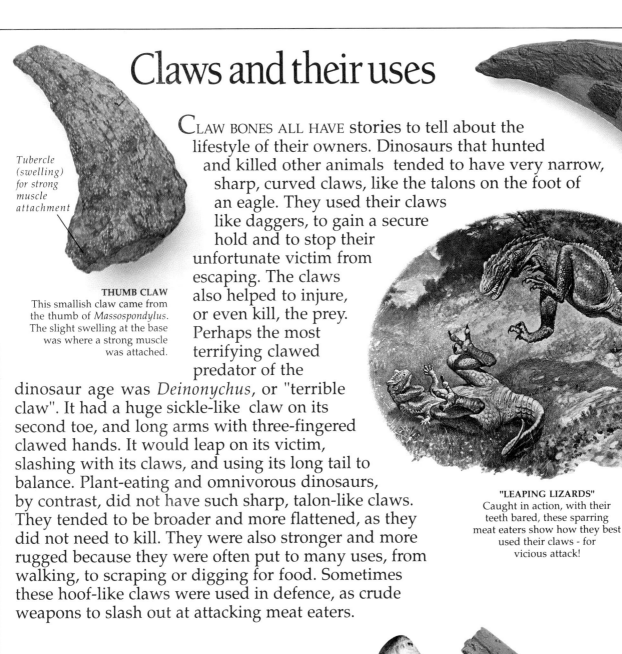

Claw BONES ALL HAVE stories to tell about the lifestyle of their owners. Dinosaurs that hunted and killed other animals tended to have very narrow, sharp, curved claws, like the talons on the foot of an eagle. They used their claws like daggers, to gain a secure hold and to stop their unfortunate victim from escaping. The claws also helped to injure, or even kill, the prey. Perhaps the most terrifying clawed predator of the dinosaur age was *Deinonychus*, or "terrible claw". It had a huge sickle-like claw on its second toe, and long arms with three-fingered clawed hands. It would leap on its victim, slashing with its claws, and using its long tail to balance. Plant-eating and omnivorous dinosaurs, by contrast, did not have such sharp, talon-like claws. They tended to be broader and more flattened, as they did not need to kill. They were also stronger and more rugged because they were often put to many uses, from walking, to scraping or digging for food. Sometimes these hoof-like claws were used in defence, as crude weapons to slash out at attacking meat eaters.

Tubercle (swelling) for strong muscle attachment

THUMB CLAW
This smallish claw came from the thumb of *Massospondylus*. The slight swelling at the base was where a strong muscle was attached.

"LEAPING LIZARDS"
Caught in action, with their teeth bared, these sparring meat eaters show how they best used their claws - for vicious attack!

ROAD RUNNER
From the picture it is easy to see why this dinosaur is called *Ornithomimus*, or ostrich dinosaur. Its main power lay in its long legs, which gave it the speed to beat a hasty retreat from pursuers, or to chase insects and small mammals. It probably used its claws and long fingers to search for food, or to scrabble in the earth for other dinosaurs' eggs.

Flattened claw

NOT FOR ATTACK
Although *Ornithomimus* was a meat eater, its claws were quite flattened, and would not have been much use for defence or attack.

FISHING TACKLE
This hand claw was found only recently in Britain, along with other remains of a meat-eating dinosaur (pp. 54-55). The remarkable size and shape of the claw earned the newly discovered dinosaur the nickname "Claws". A flesh eater, it may have used its highly curved claw like a harpoon, to catch fish for its dinner!

ELEPHANT FEET
This huge claw came from a relative of *Diplodocus* (pp. 14-21), called *Apatosaurus*. A plant eater, it walked on four, pillar-like legs and had rounded feet, like an elephant's. Most of its claws were short and hoof-like, except for the inside one on the front foot, shown here. This claw may have been used for digging, or even for defence.

Groove where horny covering was attached to claw

Rough bone for attachment of heavy claw horn

Baryonyx claw

FIGHTING TOOTH AND NAIL
Agile and intelligent, *Deinonychus* males may have fought over females or territory, as shown here. Their stiff, bony tails were useful for balancing while leaping, or pursuing a victim (p. 19).

43

Eggs and nests

DINOSAURS, LIKE REPTILES AND BIRDS today, laid hard-shelled eggs. We know this because many fossilized dinosaur eggs have been found, some even containing small skeletons. Sometimes the eggs have been found in nests, with remains of the parent dinosaurs nearby. Nests found complete with fossilized young tell us that baby dinosaurs, like baby birds, would instinctively stay in their nest, no matter what happened to their mother. Several nests found close together suggest that some dinosaurs nested in colonies. It is perhaps surprising that dinosaur eggs were never very huge. If they were in proportion to the size of some adult dinosaurs, the shells would have been far too thick to hatch, and would not have allowed enough oxygen to reach the creatures growing inside.

A baby *Maiasaura* (p. 46) emerges from its egg

Cracks which occurred during fossilization

Protoceratops egg

Unidentified dinosaur egg

Quail egg

BIRD AND DINOSAUR
When you consider that this quail's egg (left), would have hatched into a little bird, while the dinosaur egg (right) would have hatched into a massive creature, the size difference is not really so great!

Textured dinosaur eggshell

SPIKED LIZARD
Styracosaurus or "spiked lizard" was one of the bigger ceratopians. *Protoceratops*, one of the earliest of the ceratopian group, did not have any true horns, and would only have reached this dinosaur's knee (p. 46).

A HARD SHEL
This elongate egg was laid by *Protoceratops*, one a group of dinosau called ceratopians (p 30-31). Found in Mongoli in the 1920s, it was part the first evidence that dinosau laid eggs. They laid their eggs on lan just like lizards do today. The amphibian from which they evolved, had to lay their eg in water, where they hatched into tadpoles. Reptile however, can lay their eggs on land because the egg have tough shells with a private pond inside for th young to develop safely. Laying eggs like this wa probably one of the reasons why the dinosau survived on Earth for so lon

A BEAST'S NEST
The eggs in this sandy nest came from a *Protoceratops*. Several mothers laid their eggs in a circle in the same nest, which contained up to 30 eggs. They would then have covered them with earth or sand to protect them until they hatched. Fossils of baby, juvenile, and adult *Protoceratops* have been found close together, which suggests they may have lived in family groups. Some dinosaur nests, like those built by the duckbills (p. 28), had raised rims, and these mothers might have sat on their eggs, just like brooding hens!

st in which eggs
re buried has turned
) sandstone through
silization process

Birth and growth

BECAUSE MOST OF the dinosaurs were so big, it is hard to imagine them as going through baby and juvenile, as well as adult stages in their lives. But recent discoveries have enabled us to piece together a little of their early lives. We know that dinosaur mothers laid their eggs in hollowed-out nests in the ground (pp. 44-45). In some cases, tiny skeletons of hatchlings have been found inside the eggs. Colonies of duckbill dinosaur nests have been found containing skeletons of hatchlings. Their teeth are worn, indicating that the mother dinosaur would have brought food back to the nest. Baby dinosaurs probably grew fast. In the case of sauropods, which moved in herds (p. 12), the youngsters probably walked in the middle, protected by the adults on the outside. Some dinosaurs, like the ceratopians, changed their bodily proportions as they grew up.

THE NURSERY
Protoceratops (p. 45) laid their eggs in communal nests of 20 or more eggs, arranged in circles. This family scene shows baby *Protoceratops* at various stages - some hatching, some taking the first steps, and some struggling to get out of the sand!

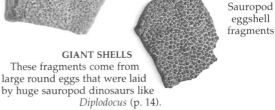

Nostril   *Flattened nose ridge*   *Orbit (eye socket)*

Nostri

Sauropod eggshell fragments

GIANT SHELLS
These fragments come from large round eggs that were laid by huge sauropod dinosaurs like *Diplodocus* (p. 14).

A BEAST EMERGES
This fossilized eggshell (left) contains a hatchling duckbill dinosaur called *Maiasaura*, or "good mother lizard". It was found recently in Montana, USA, along with hundreds of other dinosaur eggs and babies. It is shown here at life-size - small enough to fit in an adult's hand.

Protoceratops eggshell fragments

COARSE SHELLS
The coarse, pimply surface of these *Protoceratops* shell fragment is typical of many dinosaur eggs.

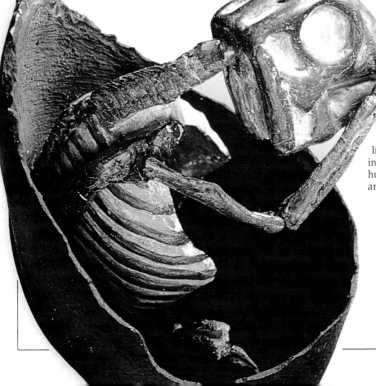

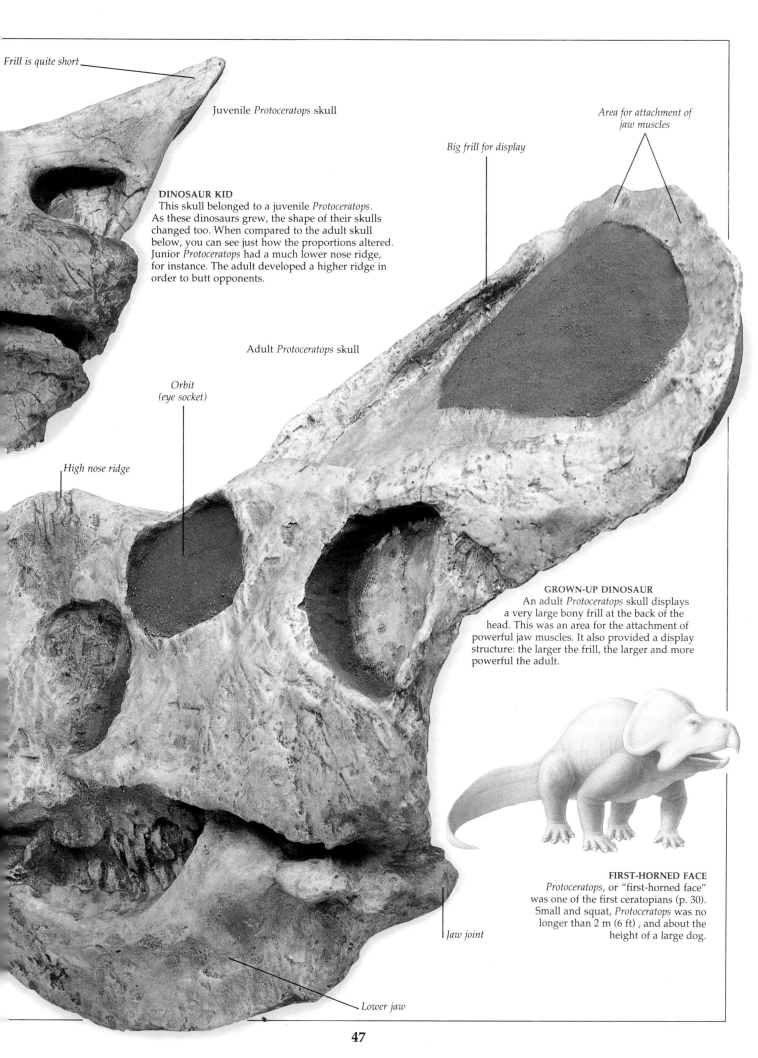

Frill is quite short

Juvenile *Protoceratops* skull

Big frill for display

Area for attachment of
jaw muscles

DINOSAUR KID
This skull belonged to a juvenile *Protoceratops*.
As these dinosaurs grew, the shape of their skulls
changed too. When compared to the adult skull
below, you can see just how the proportions altered.
Junior *Protoceratops* had a much lower nose ridge,
for instance. The adult developed a higher ridge in
order to butt opponents.

Adult *Protoceratops* skull

Orbit
(eye socket)

High nose ridge

GROWN-UP DINOSAUR
An adult *Protoceratops* skull displays
a very large bony frill at the back of the
head. This was an area for the attachment of
powerful jaw muscles. It also provided a display
structure: the larger the frill, the larger and more
powerful the adult.

FIRST-HORNED FACE
Protoceratops, or "first-horned face"
was one of the first ceratopians (p. 30).
Small and squat, *Protoceratops* was no
longer than 2 m (6 ft) , and about the
height of a large dog.

Jaw joint

Lower jaw

Death of the dinosaurs

DINOSAURS DISAPPEARED from the Earth quite suddenly, and why this happened is still a mystery. Around 70 million years ago, the dinosaurs ruled the Earth. Yet about five million years later, they had all died out, perhaps only in a matter of months. Scientists have put forward various theories to explain their sudden extinction, but many ignore one vital point: dinosaurs were only one of a whole range of creatures that died out at the same time, including all the swimming and flying reptiles. So any theory to explain dinosaur extinction must explain the disappearance of these groups as well. The theories are numerous: some people think that small mammals ate all the dinosaur eggs. This is very unlikely - for how would it account for the extinction of other species that disappeared at the same time? Others believe that dinosaurs simply grew tired of life on Earth and died of boredom!

POISONOUS BITE
It has been suggested that dinosaurs died out because they ate new kinds of poisonous plants, such as deadly nightshade, that started growing on the Earth.

Stony meteorite fragment

ROCKS FROM SPACE
A likely reason for the sudden extinction is that a massive meteorite from space collided with the Earth. This would have been catastrophic, causing a huge steam and dust cloud which darkened the Earth for a long time, killing off the plants and the animals that fed on them.

Fossilized ammonite

Iron meteorite fragment

A MASS EXTINCTION
Many other creatures died out at the time of the dinosaur extinction. Whatever happened seemed to affect some creatures, while leaving others unscathed. Ammonites, a type of shellfish, became extinct, as did the mosasaurs, plesiosaurs, and ichthyosaurs, groups of meat-eating marine reptiles. Sea crocodiles died out but the river crocodiles survived. The flying reptiles, pterosaurs, disappeared, but birds were unaffected.

Iguanodon ischium (hip bone)

Shaft of ischium bent forward after repair

Section of
hadrosaur backbone

*Vertebral
spine*

**THE BEGINNING
OF THE END**
A *Tyrannosaurus rex*
is shown fleeing in
terror as a meteor hits
the Earth. The impact
would have had an effect
rather like that of a massive
nuclear war. Dense black clouds of dust and
soot would have cut out the sun for months.

A GROWTH
Dinosaurs could contract cancer. This section of backbone
belonged to a hadrosaur, and shows a swollen area
which was a cancerous tumour in the bone.

*Point of
fracture*

*Thickening of
bone around break*

*Vertebral
body*

*Swollen area of
tumour growth*

BROKEN BONE
During their reign, dinosaurs were not immune to diseases
and accidents. The *Iguanodon* hip bone (above), shows a fracture
that healed itself during the creature's lifetime.

Dinosaur or bird?

ARE BIRDS THE DESCENDANTS of the dinosaurs? Until about sixty years ago, experts disregarded any such relationship. This was largely because they assumed that dinosaurs did not have a wishbone, and therefore could never have evolved into birds, which have a very well-developed one. The wishbone in birds helps to keep the wing joint in position. Now, however, we know that several dinosaurs - mainly meat eaters - actually did have a wishbone. Much of the debate surrounds a fossil bird called *Archaeopteryx*, or "ancient wing", which lived 150 million years ago, alongside the dinosaurs. It certainly had feathers, like all birds, but it also had many reptilian features, like teeth, for instance, unknown in modern birds. An American professor who studied *Archaeopteryx* very carefully, found that it shared over 20 features with meat-eating dinosaurs like *Coelophysis*, below. So was *Archaeopteryx* a bird, or a dinosaur with feathers? And is it the link between dinosaurs and the birds of today? The debate continues.

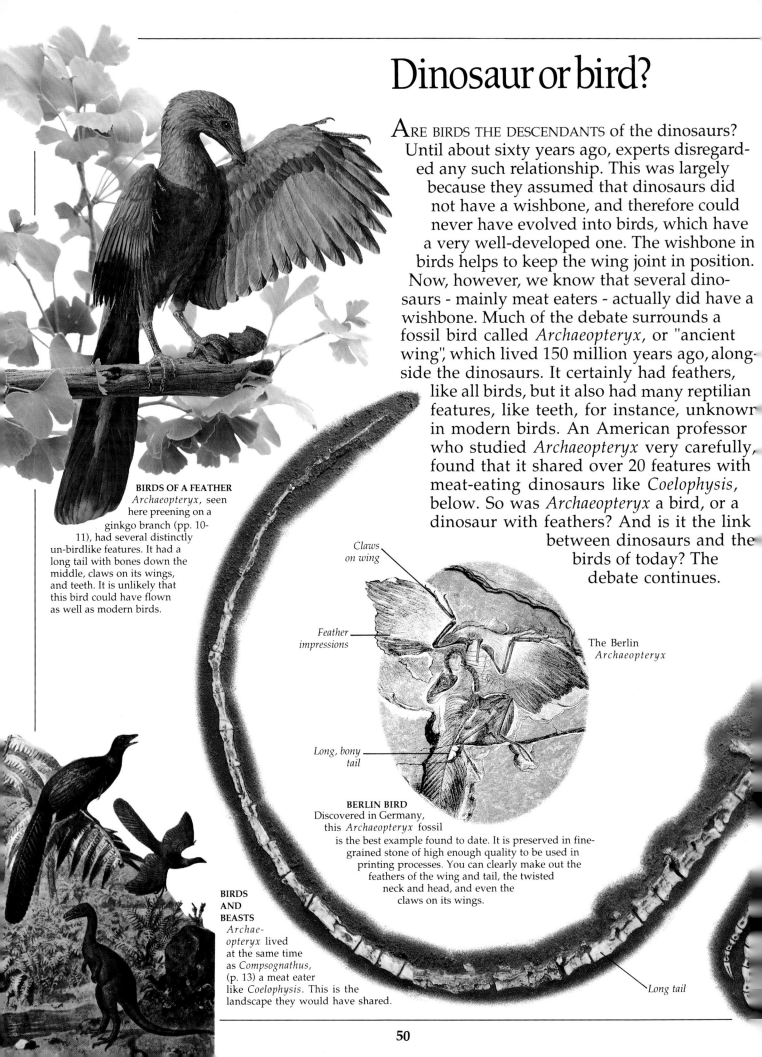

BIRDS OF A FEATHER
Archaeopteryx, seen here preening on a ginkgo branch (pp. 10-11), had several distinctly un-birdlike features. It had a long tail with bones down the middle, claws on its wings, and teeth. It is unlikely that this bird could have flown as well as modern birds.

Claws on wing

Feather impressions

Long, bony tail

The Berlin *Archaeopteryx*

BERLIN BIRD
Discovered in Germany, this *Archaeopteryx* fossil is the best example found to date. It is preserved in fine-grained stone of high enough quality to be used in printing processes. You can clearly make out the feathers of the wing and tail, the twisted neck and head, and even the claws on its wings.

BIRDS AND BEASTS
Archaeopteryx lived at the same time as *Compsognathus*, (p. 13) a meat eater like *Coelophysis*. This is the landscape they would have shared.

Long tail

FOSSIL FABLE
This complete fossil of *Coelophysis*, a small meat-eating dinosaur, was found at Ghost Ranch in Texas, USA, along with many others. It lived right at the beginning of the dinosaur age. Lightly built and agile, it had three strong clawed fingers on each hand - another feature in common with *Archaeopteryx*. In its belly you can see bones that are actually the remains of some young of the same species. So *Coelophysis* may have been a cannibal.

Coelophysis skeleton

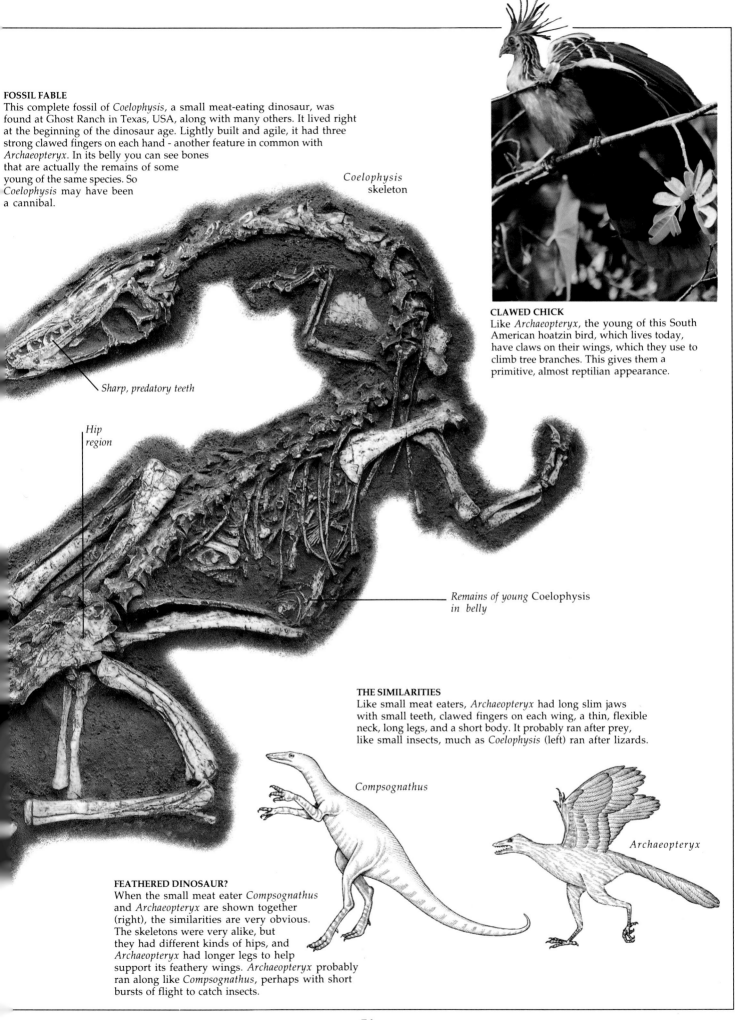

Sharp, predatory teeth

Hip region

Remains of young Coelophysis *in belly*

CLAWED CHICK
Like *Archaeopteryx*, the young of this South American hoatzin bird, which lives today, have claws on their wings, which they use to climb tree branches. This gives them a primitive, almost reptilian appearance.

THE SIMILARITIES
Like small meat eaters, *Archaeopteryx* had long slim jaws with small teeth, clawed fingers on each wing, a thin, flexible neck, long legs, and a short body. It probably ran after prey, like small insects, much as *Coelophysis* (left) ran after lizards.

Compsognathus

Archaeopteryx

FEATHERED DINOSAUR?
When the small meat eater *Compsognathus* and *Archaeopteryx* are shown together (right), the similarities are very obvious. The skeletons were very alike, but they had different kinds of hips, and *Archaeopteryx* had longer legs to help support its feathery wings. *Archaeopteryx* probably ran along like *Compsognathus*, perhaps with short bursts of flight to catch insects.

51

How to find a dinosaur

HOW DO SCIENTISTS go about discovering dinosaur remains? Because the dinosaurs became fossilized in the first place by being buried in sand, or mud, we know that their fossils can only be found in sedimentary rock - rock that has been built up in layers over the years. Fossils are often found by accident, by builders, or quarrymen digging into the ground. Fossil collectors may set out deliberately to search an area that is thought to be rich in fossils. Sometimes a large and highly organized scientific expedition is undertaken, based on detailed research. Whatever the method of discovery, careful preparation must be done if the find is to be recovered successfully. Records need to be made of the exact position of the find, and the right tools are needed to ensure that the fossils are extracted from the site and returned to the laboratory without being damaged.

THE FIND!
Discoveries of fossil dinosaurs are rare, and best tackled by a team of experienced people.

DUTCH DISCOVERY
The jaws of the mighty sea lizard *Mosasaurus* were discovered deep in a chalk mine near Maastricht in Holland in 1770. This etching shows the team of discoverers working by torchlight.

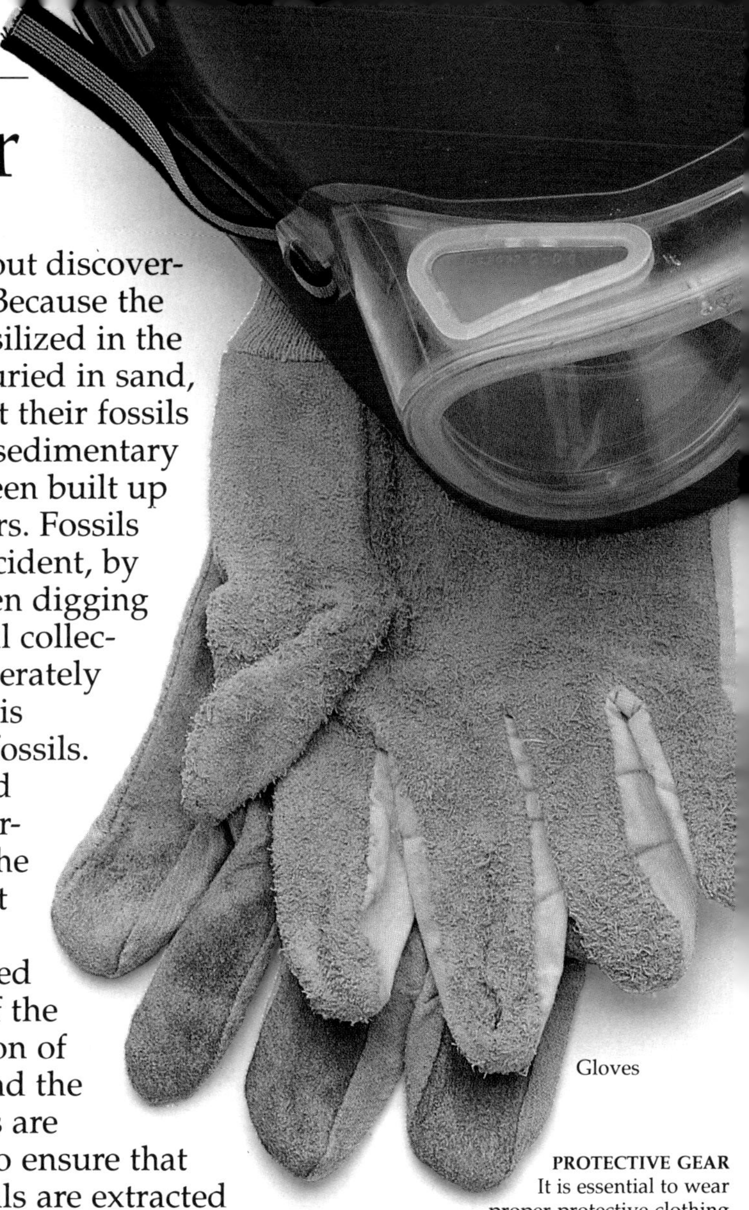

Gloves

PROTECTIVE GEAR
It is essential to wear proper protective clothing while on a fossil dig. Gloves are needed where heavy hammering and chiselling is to be done, as are goggles to prevent splinters of rock from damaging the eyes. A hard hat is also advisable, especially if work is being done near cliffs.

TAKING NOTE
On a dig, palaeontologists always record details of a find, and draw a map of the site. Broken fragments and samples of rock are collected in bags and analysed later back in the laboratory.

HAMMERS
A variety of hammers are used by palaeontologists (fossil experts) in the field. The geological hammers shown here are good at splitting fossil-bearing rock.

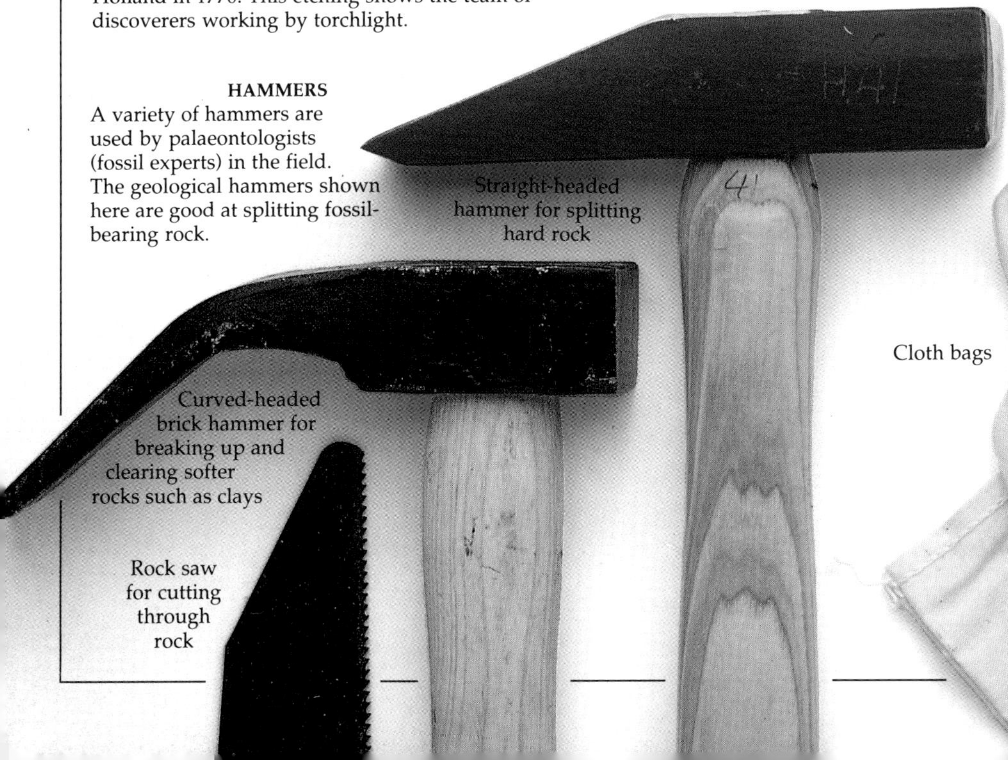

Straight-headed hammer for splitting hard rock

Cloth bags

Curved-headed brick hammer for breaking up and clearing softer rocks such as clays

Rock saw for cutting through rock

Hard hat and
protective goggles

Pointed chisels

Flat chisels

Plastic
bags

Lump hammer

Soft
paintbrush

Hard paintbrush

Pot of glue

Clipboard with
drawing of the
site, and notebook
with field notes

RIBS IN A JACKET
When fossils are partly
exposed, they are sometimes
encased in plaster jackets to
protect them for transportation
back to the laboratory. Two
ribs of the recently discovered
dinosaur *Baryonyx* can be seen
in this jacket (pp. 54-55).

POT AND BRUSHES
Brushes are used to clear
away dust while rock is
being chipped away
around fossils. As a fossil
is exposed, it is often
painted with hardener,
like glue, to secure any
loose fragments.

EXPOSING A FIND
When the rock in
which the fossil is
embedded is very
hard, a heavy hammer
and chisels are needed.
This lump hammer is
used to drive chisels into
the rock. It is useful to
have a wide variety of
chisels for getting into
awkward corners.

PROTECTING THE FIND
A palaeontologist on a dig
carefully covers a fossil with
a plaster jacket.

Baryonyx ribs
encased in plaster jacket

*Aluminium foil
covers fossil*

FOAM JACKET
Sometimes fossils are protected by
a polyurethane foam jacket. The
fossil is first wrapped in foil, then
the chemicals to make the foam are poured
over it. The foam expands and surrounds the
fossil, which can then be moved safely.
CAUTION: Foam gives off toxic gases as it
is mixed, and is not recommended for use
except by professionals.

Polyurethane
foam jacket

RAW MATERIALS
To make a plaster jacket, the plaster
is mixed with water to make a paste,
then the scrim is dipped into it. A
layer of wet tissue paper is used to
cover the rock and fossil before
plaster and scrim is applied. This
prevents the plaster sticking to
the rock and fossil.

Roll of plasterer's scrim
(open-weave fabric),
and plaster of Paris

How to rebuild a dinosaur

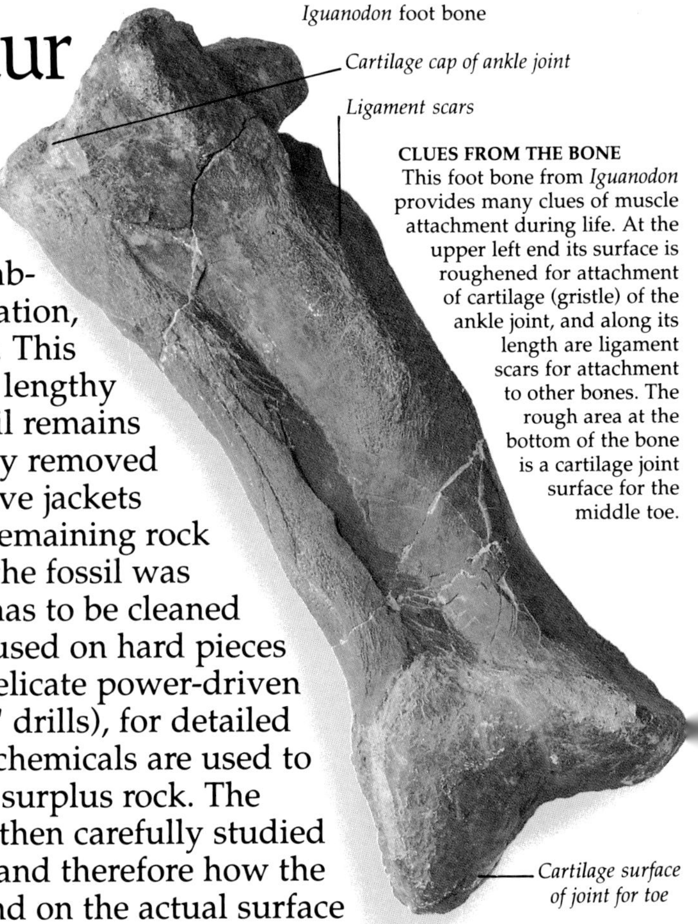

AFTER THE hard work of excavation, the precious fossils are taken back to the laboratory for preparation, study, and display. This whole process is a lengthy one. First, the fossil remains need to be carefully removed from their protective jackets (p. 53). Then, the remaining rock or earth in which the fossil was originally buried has to be cleaned away. Chisels are used on hard pieces of rock, or more delicate power-driven tools (like dentists' drills), for detailed work. Sometimes chemicals are used to dissolve away the surplus rock. The cleaned bones are then carefully studied in order to understand how they fitted together, and therefore how the dinosaur lived. Some tell-tale clues are to be found on the actual surface of bones, because muscles sometimes leave clear marks where they were attached. These marks can be used to reconstruct dinosaur muscles.

READY TO DISPLAY
The laboratory workers shown here are putting the finishing touches to what has probably been months, or even years, of work cleaning and preparing this fossil skeleton.

Iguanodon foot bone

Cartilage cap of ankle joint

Ligament scars

CLUES FROM THE BONE
This foot bone from *Iguanodon* provides many clues of muscle attachment during life. At the upper left end its surface is roughened for attachment of cartilage (gristle) of the ankle joint, and along its length are ligament scars for attachment to other bones. The rough area at the bottom of the bone is a cartilage joint surface for the middle toe.

Cartilage surface of joint for toe

Adding the flesh

Once all the bones of the dinosaur's skeleton have been cleaned, scientists can attempt a reconstruction of the body. It may take some time to work out how the bones fitted together, and missing bones may have to be modelled from plaster. Then the "flesh" can be added, based on detailed knowledge of how the dinosaur's muscles were arranged. This is established by studying "muscle scars" on the bones, and comparing them with the bones of living reptiles.

FINISHING TOUCH
Many hours of work in the field and laboratory by scientists, and finally the model-maker have gone into the fleshed-out dinosaur model shown here.

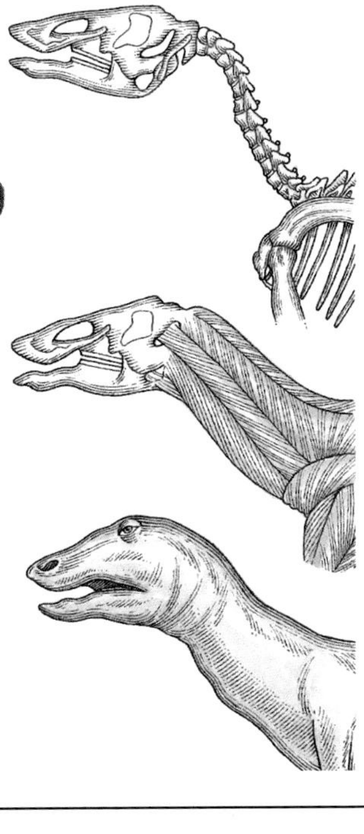

RECONSTRUCTED SKELETON
Once the skeleton has been put together, an attempt at fleshing out the dinosaur can begin. A special scientific artist makes sketches to help the model-maker.

MUSCLING IN
By studying the bones the muscles can be added as accurately as possible.

ADDING THE SKIN
Finally, the skin is added. This is more difficult, but skin impressions are sometimes preserved (p. 32). Colour is a matter of guesswork.

Baryonyx neck
vertebra

Faint
scratches

A LOAD OF OLD BONES
During the 19th century, when dinosaurs had just been
discovered, (pp. 8-9), the sculptor Benjamin Waterhouse
Hawkins built models of dinosaurs first in Britain,
then in the United States. This shows his work-
shop in New York.

A NECK BONE
This neck bone
belonged to the
newly discovered dinosaur
Baryonyx, seen reconstructed
below. The bone has a
very complicated shape and
was buried in very hard rock,
so it took a very long time to
prepare. The faint scratches
that can be seen are where
rock remains to be cleared.

AN ACID BATH
Sometimes, in laboratories,
vats of acid are used to dissolve away rock from fossils
without damaging them. The
chemicals used in this process
can be very dangerous, so protective clothing must always be worn
when lowering the fossil into the vat.

IN DEATH THROES
Baryonyx is shown here as it looked
after it died. It sank to the bottom
of a lake where it gradually
became fossilized. Such a
realistic model shows how
the skills of the scientist
and model-maker can be
brought together to great
effect. The way that
the dinosaur was lying
was worked out from
the position in which
the bones were found.

Model of *Baryonyx* as it looked after it died

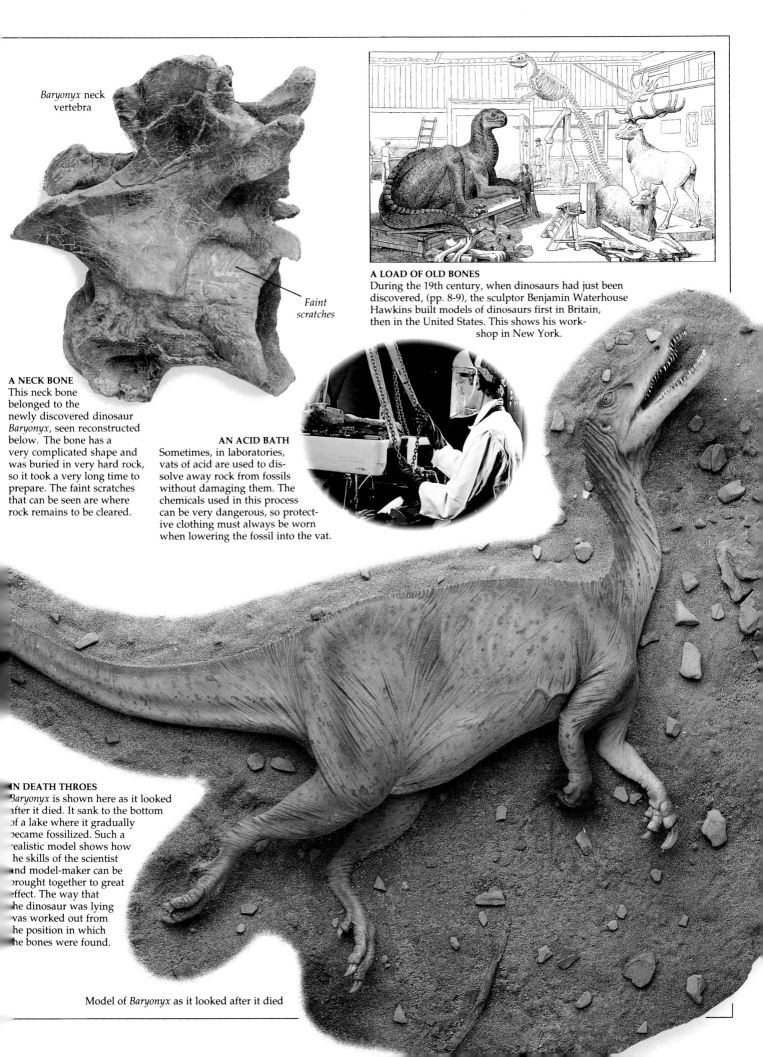

The timescale

TRILOBITE
This creature lived on the sea bed and scuttled around on sharp, spiny legs. Although abundant in the early oceans, it was extinct long before the first dinosaurs appeared.

I[T IS INCREDIBLE TO THINK] that animals and plants have lived on this Earth for over 700 million years. During this time a bewildering variety has come and gone. The first dinosaurs appeared about 210 million years ago (mya) at the end of what is known as the Triassic Period. They roamed the Earth throughout the Jurassic Period until 64 million years ago, right at the end of the Cretaceous Period. During the millions of years of life on Earth, the world has changed enormously: continents have moved, sea levels have altered, climates have changed, creatures have become extinct. If we look at fossils of creatures that lived before, during, and after the dinosaur age, we can see how some things have changed, and some have remained much the same.

IN THE MISTS OF TIME
This is what the world may have looked like during the dinosaur age. Dinosaurs lived through three periods of time: the Triassic, from 230 to 195 mya, the Jurassic, from 195 to 141 mya, and the Cretaceous, from 141 to 65 mya.

At the time when the dinosaurs appeared, none of the countries of the world existed as we know them - the world consisted of one huge landmass called Pangaea.

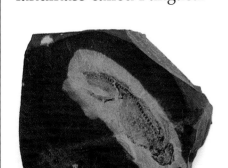

■ **260 mya:**
AMPHIBIAN
Amphibians lived before and during the dinosaur age, and are still with us today. Frogs, for instance, are amphibians. They can breathe and move on land, but have to lay their eggs in water (p. 44).

SCORPION STORY
Living scorpions belong to an ancient group which dates back about 400 million years.

Small spiky teeth

■ **260 mya:**
EARLY REPTILE
This is the underside of the skull of an early lizard-like reptile, called *Captorhinus*. It may have eaten small insects and snails with its small spiky teeth.

A BEETLE
Beetles are a group with a very long history, and were probably the prey of early reptiles and amphibians, just as they are today.

■ **230 mya:**
DIICTODON
Squat and pig-shaped, the owner of this mammal-like reptile skull ate plants and lived during the early Triassic Period.

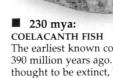

■ **230 mya:**
COELACANTH FISH
The earliest known coelacanth appeared 390 million years ago. They were thought to be extinct, but recently many living coelacanths have been discovered.

■ **230 mya:**
PROCOLOPHON
This is the skull of a small early reptile which fed on roots and tubers.

Spaces for jaw muscles

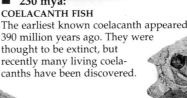

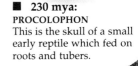

LIVING FOSSIL
This lungfish has fossil relatives which date back 390 million years.

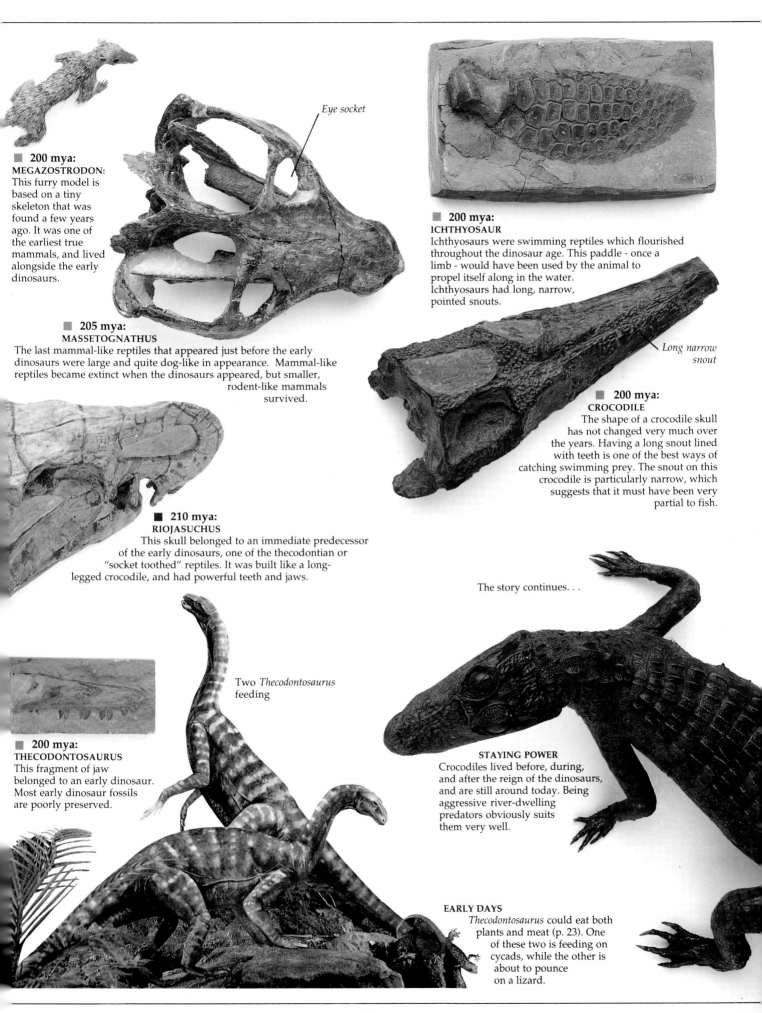

200 mya:
MEGAZOSTRODON:
This furry model is based on a tiny skeleton that was found a few years ago. It was one of the earliest true mammals, and lived alongside the early dinosaurs.

Eye socket

205 mya:
MASSETOGNATHUS
The last mammal-like reptiles that appeared just before the early dinosaurs were large and quite dog-like in appearance. Mammal-like reptiles became extinct when the dinosaurs appeared, but smaller, rodent-like mammals survived.

210 mya:
RIOJASUCHUS
This skull belonged to an immediate predecessor of the early dinosaurs, one of the thecodontian or "socket toothed" reptiles. It was built like a long-legged crocodile, and had powerful teeth and jaws.

200 mya:
THECODONTOSAURUS
This fragment of jaw belonged to an early dinosaur. Most early dinosaur fossils are poorly preserved.

Two *Thecodontosaurus* feeding

200 mya:
ICHTHYOSAUR
Ichthyosaurs were swimming reptiles which flourished throughout the dinosaur age. This paddle - once a limb - would have been used by the animal to propel itself along in the water. Ichthyosaurs had long, narrow, pointed snouts.

Long narrow snout

200 mya:
CROCODILE
The shape of a crocodile skull has not changed very much over the years. Having a long snout lined with teeth is one of the best ways of catching swimming prey. The snout on this crocodile is particularly narrow, which suggests that it must have been very partial to fish.

The story continues. . .

STAYING POWER
Crocodiles lived before, during, and after the reign of the dinosaurs, and are still around today. Being aggressive river-dwelling predators obviously suits them very well.

EARLY DAYS
Thecodontosaurus could eat both plants and meat (p. 23). One of these two is feeding on cycads, while the other is about to pounce on a lizard.

57

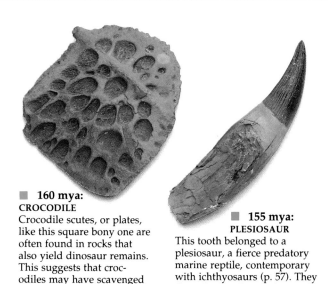

160 mya:
CROCODILE
Crocodile scutes, or plates, like this square bony one are often found in rocks that also yield dinosaur remains. This suggests that crocodiles may have scavenged dinosaur carcasses.

155 mya:
PLESIOSAUR
This tooth belonged to a plesiosaur, a fierce predatory marine reptile, contemporary with ichthyosaurs (p. 57). They flourished in the sea during the Jurassic Period.

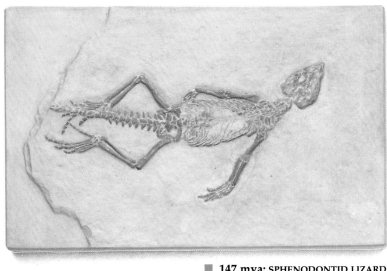

147 mya: SPHENODONTID LIZARD
Lizard-like reptiles such as this specimen have a very long history. They lived throughout the reign of the dinosaurs.

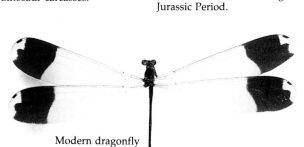

Modern dragonfly

Fossil dragonfly

140 mya:
DATED DRAGONFLY
Dragonflies can be called "living fossils": they were flying in the skies 320 million years ago, and still exist today.

140 mya:
KING CRAB
King crabs are only remotely related to crabs. They have been around since before the dinosaur age, and still live today.

140 mya:
GRYODUS
Many types of bony fish like this one lived at the same time as the dinosaurs. Most were fossilized in fine lake sediments, so are preserved in great detail.

Grey plover

DAWN OF THE BIRDS
The first birds appeared in the late Jurassic Period - about 150 mya. But they did not come into their own and dominate the skies until the pterosaurs became extinct (at the same time as the dinosaurs).

145 mya:
PTERODACTYLUS
Flying reptiles called pterosaurs flew in the skies while the dinosaurs ruled the land. Some were the size of sparrows; others were as big as small aircraft. The larger ones would have swooped down to catch fish in the waters, while smaller ones, like this *Pterodactylus* (right), would have caught insects in the air.

COME FLY. . .
In the Jurassic Period, a sky scene at dawn or dusk would have been crowded with pterosaurs darting through the air catching prey. Their place is taken today by birds that feed on the wing: swifts, housemartins, and swallows.

THE GREAT SURVIVOR
The cockroach is one of Nature's great survivors. Cockroaches have lived on Earth since long before the dinosaur age, and, judging by their success at living in human environments, they seem set to survive well into the future.

Cockroach

Water moccasin snake

SNAKES ON THE SCENE
Slithering snakes arrived on the scene in the late Cretaceous Period. They are like modified legless lizards.

■ **136 mya:**
DRYOSAURUS
This femur (thigh bone) belonged to a small, fast-moving, plant-eating dinosaur. It used its speed to flee fierce predators.

Dryosaurus femur

■ **120 mya:**
LIZARD'S JAW
This fragment of jaw came from a lizard like the sphenodontid preserved in rock, above left. Fragments like this are found more often than complete specimens.

■ **120 mya:**
CROCODILE
The crocodile that owned this skull (right) lived in the early Cretaceous Period.

■ **115 mya:**
IGUANODON
This is a tail bone from *Iguanodon*, a plant-eating dinosaur (pp. 8-9). *Iguanodon* lived only in the Cretaceous Period.

■ **120 mya: TEETH**
These fierce-looking stumpy crocodile teeth are preserved from 120 million years ago, but are very like the teeth that belong to living crocodiles today.

The story continues. . .

■ **120 mya:**
SCUTE
Part of a crocodile's bony armour, this scute comes from a crocodile that lived during the Cretaceous Period.

■ **110 mya:**
GASTROPOD
Many different snails lived during the dinosaur age.

The end of an era

As THE CRETACEOUS PERIOD drew to a close, the dinosaurs became gradually less numerous, until eventually they disappeared altogether. At the same time changes were also taking place in the Earth's landscape. The continents became separated by wide stretches of sea. Sea levels rose also, flooding much of the low-lying land where many types of dinosaur lived. Many groups of sea animals became extinct. Instead of being warm all the time, the climate began to become more variable, or seasonal. The types of plants living at the time also changed: flowering plants became increasingly important. As the dinosaurs died out, they made way for a new ruling group on the Earth: the mammals.

NOT LONG TO LIVE
The formidable mosasaurs only lived at the end of the Cretaceous Period, and became extinct alongside the dinosaurs.

■ **70 mya:**
MOSASAUR
This giant marine lizard used its large pointed teeth to crack open shells of animals such as ammonites (p. 48).

Turtle shell

■ **95 mya:**
TURTLE
This turtle shell is a relic from the Cretaceous Period. Turtles were another group that flourished instead of becoming extinct.

■ **90 mya:**
ALBERTOSAURUS
The owner of this toe bone was a large meat-eating dinosaur. Few of these meat eaters survived up to the end of the dinosaur age.

■ **100 mya:**
ICHTHYOSAUR
Embedded in rock, these sharp, pointed teeth belonged to an ichthyosaur (p. 57). Marine reptiles like this all became extinct at the same time as the dinosaurs.

Scales

■ **75 mya:**
CRAB
Closely related to the lobsters, crabs did not suffer extinction (p. 58).

Crab

■ **85 mya:**
MARSUPIAL
This jaw bone belonged to a pouched mammal (like a kangaroo). Now found only in Australia, marsupials lived alongside the dinosaurs, and were able to evolve rapidly after they disappeared.

■ **90 mya:**
BONY FISH
Bony ray-finned fish were another group that suffered very little damage during the "great extinction".

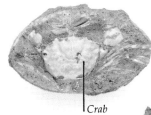

■ **100 mya:**
LOBSTER
Some marine groups, like the lobsters, were little affected by the mass extinction that happened at the end of the Cretaceous Period. Why some groups were affected, and others not, is to this day a great mystery.

■ **100 mya:**
LEAF
Broad leaves like this one are typical of flowering plants that appeared during the Cretaceous Period.

RED HERRING?
The bony fish we are familiar with today are very like those that lived in the late Cretaceous.

Hawksbill turtle

TURTLE TALE
Turtles and
tortoises belong to
a group of reptiles
that have changed
very little in appearance
since their origins 200
million years ago.

55 mya:
TURTLE SKULL

Spider

Cricket

Hyracotherium
(early horse) skull

25 mya:
SHARK TOOTH
Sharks have been
around for 400
million years,
and have
changed
very little.

35 mya:
INSECTS IN AMBER
This cricket and
spider have been
perfectly preserved
from millions of years ago,
because they became trapped
in amber (fossilized resin)
exuding from
pine trees.

Early rodent skull

35 mya:
EARLY RODENT
Gnawing animals like rats and
mice did not exist until well
after the dinosaurs died, and
are thriving today.

40 mya:
LIZARD
This jaw belonged to a
land lizard. Although all
the giant marine lizards like
mosasaurs (pp. 48 and 60)
became extinct with the
dinosaurs, the small
land-living ones were
unaffected.

50 mya:
EARLY HORSE
Horses appeared soon after the
dinosaurs became extinct, and soon
there were many different types of
horse grazing upon the new plants
and grasses that were growing.
Early horses had toes, not hooves,
on their feet.

1 mya:
HOMO ERECTUS
Human beings were one of the last
species to arrive on the ever-
changing scene on Earth. Early
species of humans date back
a mere one million years
(64 million years after
the last dinosaur died).
In this "short" period
of time, people have
risen to dominate
most of the land,
and are
beginning to
have a notice-
able effect
on the
environment.

Human skull

A BRACHIOPOD
One of the longest survivors of all
groups in nature, brachiopods,
or "lampshells", found today
are little changed from types
found in rocks 500
million years old.

Red rose

FLOWER POWER
The flowering plants that appeared
early in the Cretaceous Period soon
begin to dominate the plant world.

THE BUZZING BEGINS
Brightly coloured flowers and flower scents seemed to
herald the arrival of butterflies and bees. Attracted by
the colours and scents of the flowers, butterflies, bees,
and other insects carried pollen from one to the other, just
like they do today.

Myths and legends

WHEN DINOSAUR BONES were first discovered, people found it hard to believe that these creatures had actually lived on Earth. The giant dinosaurs became linked with terrifying monsters in peoples' minds. Because so little was known about them, many mistakes were made at the beginning. Dinosaur bones were put together in the wrong way (p. 8), or even mixed up with other bones. Today, misconceptions about dinosaurs are just as common. Visitors to museums often think that the dinosaurs walked around looking like living skeletons! Politicians and commentators sometimes unfairly use dinosaurs to describe something that is old-fashioned, out of date, useless, or inefficient. It is common to think that dinosaurs were animals that were big, dull, stupid, and headed for extinction because they were poorly designed to cope with the world in which they lived. In fact, nothing could be further from the truth. Dinosaurs were among the most elegant and sophisticated animals that the Earth has ever seen, and survived for nearly 150 million years - 75 times longer than humans have lived on Earth.

DINOSAUR DRAGON
The winged dragon of mythology looks very like some dinosaurs, except for the wings. Some people see dragons and dinosaurs as being one and the same. But the big difference is that dragons never existed!

A WATERY END
A common mistake is to believe that dinosaurs were sea monsters, possibly still lurking in the ocean depths. In fact, no dinosaur was purely sea living. The sea reptiles that shared the dinosaur world were mostly plesiosaurs and ichthyosaurs.

DINOSAURS IN THE TREES
When *Hypsilophodon*, a small, agile, plant-eating dinosaur, was first discovered, it was thought to live in trees. Indeed, it was believed to be the dinosaur equivalent of a tree kangaroo that lives in Papua New Guinea. Scientists thought its long tail helped it to balance in the trees, while special sharp toes on its feet helped it to cling to branches. Now this theory has been proved wrong. In fact, *Hypsilophodon* was a ground-dwelling dinosaur that used its stiff tail as a stabilizer while running.

THE GREAT BRONTOSAURUS HOAX
The sauropod dinosaur *Apatosaurus* used to be called *Brontosaurus* many years ago. Its almost complete skeleton was dug up, lacking only a skull. When it came to reconstructing the animal, its fossil bones got mixed up with another sauropod, *Camarasaurus*, and it appeared in museums with a short and round skull. It was not until recently that the original skull was found, proving to be very like the skull of *Diplodocus* (p. 22).

CHINESE DRAGONS

The mythical dragon is an important symbol in Chinese culture, and it seems likely that it originated from the discovery of dinosaur remains. The Chinese have been collecting dinosaur fossils for over 2,000 years, but referring to them as dragon bones. Even today "dragons' teeth" which are mostly fossil dinosaur teeth are collected and ground into powders for use as medicines, for they are thought to have healing properties.

Two *Hypsilophodon* dinosaurs perched in a tree

Special grasping toes

Balancing tail

Grasping hand to hold branch

DINOSAURS AND CAVE DWELLERS

Some films and cartoons have given the impression that dinosaurs shared the Earth with early people. In fact, dinosaurs became extinct 64 million years before the first people ever appeared on the Earth!

Index

Acknowledgements

Dorling Kindersley would like to thank:
Angela Milner and the staff of the British Museum (Natural History); Kew Gardens and Clifton Nurseries for advice and plant specimens for photography; Trevor Smith's Animal World; The Institute of Vertebrate Palaeoanthropology, Beijing, for permission to photograph Chinese dinosaurs; Brian Carter for obtaining plant specimens; Victoria Sorzano for typing; William Lindsay for advice on pages 52-53 and pages 54-55; Fred Ford and Mike Pilley of Radius Graphics; Jane Parker for the index; Richard Czapnik for design assistance; and Dave King for special photography on pages 6-7 and pages 10-11.

Picture credits
t=top, b=bottom, m=middle, l=left, r=right
ANT/ NHPA: 7tr
BBC Hulton Picture Library: 8tl, 9tm, 31t, 54tl, 54b
Richard Beales/Planet Earth Pictures: 32tl
The Bridgeman Art Library: 17bl
The British Museum (Natural History): 52tl, 52ml, 55tr
Zdenek Burian/Artia Foreign Trade Corporation: 10m, 22m, 38tl
Jane Burton/Bruce Coleman Limited: 6ml, 13br, 29ml, 34tl, 35tl, 36tl, 39tr, 43bl, 50tl, 57bl, 59tl
L. Castaneda/ The Image Bank: 15mr
Albert Dickson: 46bl
Robert Harding: 63tr
David A. Hardy/ Science Photo Library: 49tl
Arthur Hayward/Natural Science Photos: 11ml, 24tr, 29bl, 33tr, 37tr, 42bl
The Illustrated London News: 38ml, 46tl,

G. Kinns/Natural Science Photos: 30tl
Kobal Collection: 63m
Ken Lucas/ Planet Earth Pictures: 31mr
The Mansell Collection: 28tl, 42mr, 56tr,
Mary Evans Picture Library: 9bl, 9m, 12tl, 14tl, 16bl, 25ml, 34ml, 35bm, 62tl, 62bl, 62mr
David Norman: 53mr
Alan Root/ Survival Anglia Ltd: 51tr
C. A. Walker/ Natural Science Photos: 40tl

Illustrations by: Angelika Elsebach for pp. 21tr, 21mr, 21br, 36b; Sandie Hill for pp. 15ml, 20ml, 28tr, 44tr, 44bl; Mark Iley for p. 18bl; Richard Ward for pp. 23bl, 26bm, 47b; Ann Winterbotham for pp. 10tl, 15bl; John Woodcock for pp. 6tr, 7mr, 12m, 14b, 14ml 51b, 54br

Picture research by: Angela Murphy

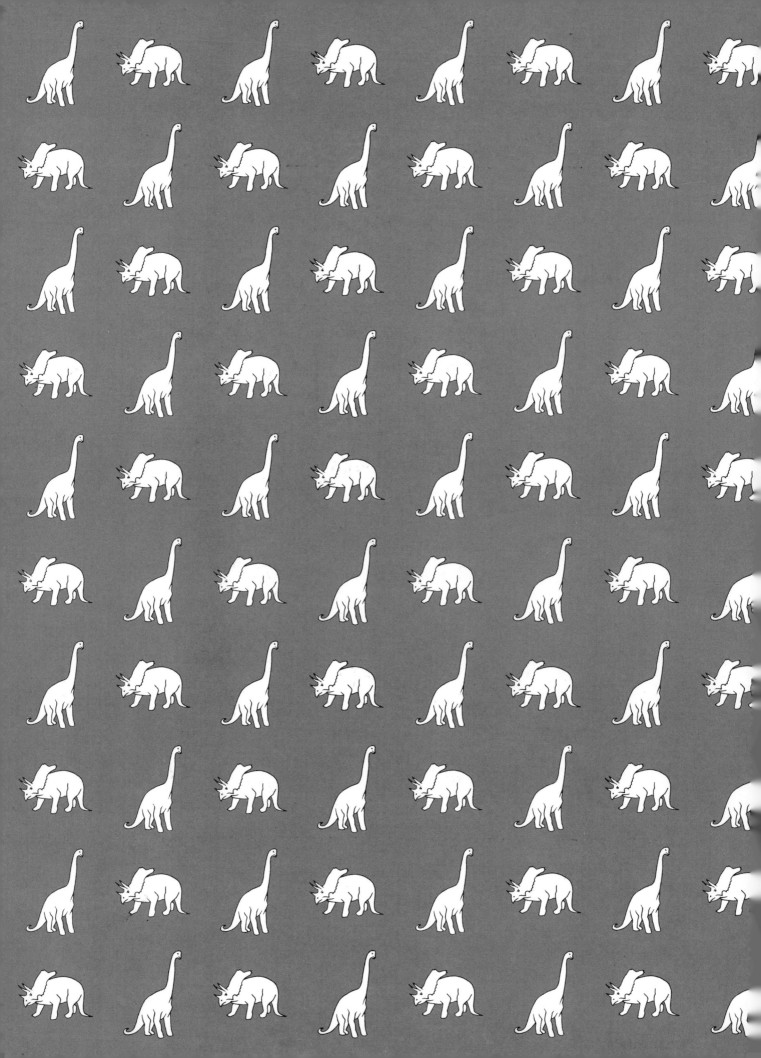